ADVANCING EQUITY

at the Intersection of Race, Mental Illness, and Criminal Justice Involvement

AF904524

Deanna M. Adams

AMERICAN BAR ASSOCIATION
Criminal Justice Section

Cover design by Elmarie Jara/ABA Design

The materials contained herein represent the opinions of the authors and/or the editors and should not be construed to be the views or opinions of the law firms or companies with whom such persons are in partnership with, associated with, or employed by, nor of the American Bar Association or the Criminal Justice Section, unless adopted pursuant to the bylaws of the Association.

Nothing contained in this book is to be considered as the rendering of legal advice for specific cases, and readers are responsible for obtaining such advice from their own legal counsel. This book is intended for educational and informational purposes only.

© 2023 American Bar Association. All rights reserved.

No part of this publication may be reproduced, stored in a retrieval system, or transmitted in any form or by any means, electronic, mechanical, photocopying, recording, or otherwise, without the prior written permission of the publisher. For permission, complete the request form at www.americanbar.org/reprint or email ABA Publishing at copyright@americanbar.org.

Printed in the United States of America.

27 26 25 24 23 5 4 3 2 1

A catalog record for this book is available from the Library of Congress.

Discounts are available for books ordered in bulk. Special consideration is given to state bars, CLE programs, and other bar-related organizations. Inquire at Book Publishing, ABA Publishing, American Bar Association, 321 N. Clark Street, Chicago, Illinois 60654-7598.

www.shopABA.org

I dedicate this book to everyone whose experience in the criminal justice system led to the need for this work.

I drew inspiration from the experiences of people involved in the criminal justice system and their hopes for equity, fairness, and justice, as well as inspiration from the attorneys, legal theorists, and scholars who are working toward equitable justice.

CONTENTS

PART III
Equity on Both Sides of the Adversarial System

PART IV
Advancing Equity across the Criminal Justice Continuum

PART V
Moving from Theory to Action

ACKNOWLEDGMENTS

Writing this book was a passion project. Equity at the intersection of criminal justice and mental health is a topic dear to my work, and one that I have had the privilege to explore and ponder with esteemed colleagues working across the legal profession, the mental health field, policymaking and legislating, law enforcement and reentry, and in other roles across the criminal justice continuum. Although there are far too many of you to name, I appreciate all that I have learned from you and look forward to our future work together.

I would like to take the time to thank Evan Marsh, LCSW, who graciously accepted eleventh-hour requests to review portions of the book and to help uncomplicate complicated mental health concepts and terminology. Thank you, Ari and Prudence Adams, for supporting me through the drafting process, and a special thank you to "Jay Doe" and "Mother Doe" whose experience with the criminal justice system lent to the conclusion of this book.

ABOUT THE AUTHOR

Deanna M. Adams has dedicated her career to improving legal and life outcomes for the people most severely impacted by the criminal justice system. She began her career working on the ground with people in jail, on probation, and on parole supervision. After years of collaborating with local criminal justice, health, and social services agencies to implement legal reforms that impacted her clients, she channeled her love for policy and implementation into providing training and technical assistance to state and local governments across the country. This work has focused on smart policy, practices, and procedures that address public safety and are responsive to people who have mental illness, co-occurring mental illness and substance use disorders, and other complex needs.

Deanna currently works for the Judicial Branch of California, the largest judiciary in the country. In addition to having worked on the ground, her previous work includes the Council of State Governments Justice Center and the Chief Probation Officers of California. She is vice-chair of the ABA Criminal Justice Section's Alternatives to Incarceration and Diversion Committee and sits on the Board of Directors of the Forensic Mental Health Association of California.

INTRODUCTION

Jurisdictions are beginning to focus criminal justice and legal reforms on reducing racial disparities. Similarly, specific responses are emerging to improve outcomes for people who have mental illness and who become involved in the justice system. It is easy to assume that these reforms make a blanket impact; however, their goals can sometimes exceed their reach. Situated between these reforms is the absent focus on people who share identities with both groups and who, without receiving specific focus, fall short of benefiting from legal reforms and fail to receive fairness and justice. This shared population is not small or underrepresented. On the contrary. This is a vast population that is both overrepresented in and disproportionately harmed by the criminal justice system. This book seeks to disrupt this injustice.

The intersection of race and mental illness is complex. Both are often pathologized, and both on their own can present unique challenges for attorneys when pursuing fair and just outcomes. When they overlap, the challenges become more complex. The disparate impact that the criminal justice system has on people who straddle these complexities is profound. Their social identities—racial demographics and mental health conditions—and the resulting inequities imposed on them are not mutually exclusive. Social identities and inequities are interdependent. Appreciating the effects of people's identities on the inequities they experience is vital. This provides the most relevant interpretation of how the criminal justice system will impact them and of where attorneys can intervene. By appreciating the effect and impact of people's identities, attorneys gain a deeper understanding of their participation in alleged crime, their responses to being witnesses or survivors of a crime, and their perception of and experience in the criminal justice system.

This book starts the conversation about what attorneys can do to improve both health and justice outcomes for people of diverse backgrounds who have mental illness. Focusing on the role of litigators working in the criminal justice system—particularly prosecutors and defense attorneys—this book offers an overview of foundational concepts, lawyering skills, and legal theories that attorneys can use in day-to-day practice as they work toward achieving fair and equitable access to justice for all.

Foundational Tenets

The ideas presented in this book follow these tenets:

- There is an understanding and acknowledgment that attorneys did not go to law school to become social workers, and that law school did not prepare attorneys to handle the social and medical needs of the people at focus of this book. Although this book draws upon concepts originally designed outside of the legal profession, the concepts describe how they have been adapted and proven successful when used by attorneys. If attorneys identify a need for social work or mental health intervention, they should make referrals to those who are appropriately qualified to provide needed services.
- The criminal justice system and legal process are complex, and there are myriad legal responses that impact people who have mental illness. This book is not making the argument that mental illness, on its own, should automatically bar criminal charges or prevent incarceration. Rather, this book advocates for attorneys to approach cases involving people who have mental illness with an eye toward therapeutic justice and using the power of the law to achieve beneficial outcomes for all parties involved in a case. This legal theory supports the concept of prioritizing treatment and rehabilitation over punishment. In the interest of public safety and public health, people who have unmet mental health needs

are better served when connected to mental health treatment instead of criminalization. When incarceration is unavoidable, people are best served when the terms and conditions of incarceration provide them with access to responsive treatment while mitigating collateral consequences of criminal convictions.

- Conversations on race, culture, and the racial frame recognize that mental health and criminal justice systems, as well as social systems at large, define white and whiteness as the default identity.[1] People often assume that everyone who interact with these systems have experiences that align with the default. The experiences of people of diverse backgrounds, however, are often significantly different from the default and often shaped by historical and structural inequities. It is the duty of attorneys to recognize and address inequities that are born into the experiences of people who interact with mental health and criminal justice systems.
- Intersectionality is a foundational concept that attorneys should understand. Introduced by legal scholar Kimberlé Crenshaw, intersectionality describes the various elements of people's identities that compound to influence different conditions of discrimination and privilege.[2] Intersectionality argues that identities—such as race, gender, disability, medical conditions, and so on—combine and interact with one another to form unique experiences of discrimination rather than acting in isolation.[3] Intersectionality should be understood in relation to its influence on crime, criminal justice involvement, legal responses, and litigation tactics.[4]

To give an idea of intersectionality, the concept acknowledges that a person who is Black + has a mental illness has a distinct experience that differs from the experience of a person who is

1. Derald Wing Sue, *The Invisible Whiteness of Being: Whiteness, White Supremacy, White Privilege, and Racism, in* Addressing racism: Facilitating cultural competence in mental health and educational settings 15 (John Wiley & Sons, Inc., 2006).

2. *Intersectionality, Merriam-Webster's Unabridged Dictionary*, https://www.merriam-webster.com/dictionary/intersectionality (last visited Mar. 27, 2022).

3. Hillary Potter, Intersectionality and Criminology: Disrupting and Revolutionizing Studies of Crime 3, 32 (Routledge, 1st ed., 2015).

4. *Id.* at 8.

white + has a mental illness. The person who is Black + has a mental illness experiences discrimination and challenges caused by (1) racism and prejudice due to their race, (2) stigma and prejudice due to having a mental illness, and (3) compounded racism, stigma, and prejudice due to them being a Black person who has a mental illness. The person who is white + has a mental illness experiences discrimination, too, because of their mental illness. However, race-based or other identity-based discrimination does not impact their experience.

Digging further into the concept, the experiences of the person who is Black + has a mental illness and the person who is white + has a mental illness are qualitatively different from someone who is Indigenous + has a mental illness, and different from someone who is Black + nonbinary + has a mental illness. Just as the compounding nature of discrimination was explored for the person who is Black + has a mental illness, the intertwining nature of discrimination for each identity held by the person who is Indigenous + has a mental illness and the person who is Black + nonbinary + has a mental illness will compound and shape their unique experiences and uniquely shape their relation to the criminal justice system.

- There is recognition of the beautiful and complex nature of race, culture, and intersectional identities. This book focuses on terminology that encompasses people of diverse backgrounds not to infer that people outside of the default background—that is, whiteness—are thereby diverse and share a collective experience. Rather, this book acknowledges that intersectional identities compound to create diverse identities and diverse experiences. This focus appreciates that discrimination and inequities are different across races and different within shared races. It recognizes the historical inequities in the criminal justice and mental health systems and acknowledges that those inequities cause deeper burdens for people of certain backgrounds.

Conversations around race and equity can be difficult. Racism and inequity can be uncomfortable topics for people who have not experienced them or who do not believe in their existence. Overshadowing this discomfort, attorneys must understand that the experiences of racism and inequity are uncomfortable, disheartening, and dehumanizing for people who experience them. Topics covered in this book may elicit complex reactions, such as guilt, anger, defensiveness, and resentment. It is not my intent to challenge anyone's lawyering ability or to accuse anyone of being racist or of lacking objectivity. Nor am I seeking to push a political agenda, or to alienate white people or whiteness in favor of multiculturalism. I wrote this book instead to provide information that assists attorneys in developing tangible skills and a conceptual framework for working on cases involving people of diverse backgrounds who have mental illness. This focus recognizes that their experiences with the criminal justice system and the legal process are often divergent from what attorneys expect, and that these divergent experiences lead to inequitable—and thus unequal—access under law.

Terminology Used throughout This Book

Race, culture, and identities are complicated. The terminology used in this book intentionally moves away from hyphenated identities that reference people's race or ethnicity with their nationality or citizenship. Hyphenated identities assume a default identify. Hyphenated identities assume the notion of otherness, which prejudices the hyphenated sociocultural identities as not belonging.[5]

Great thought went into what terminology would best describe the population at the focus of this book. What is the best term to use—people of color (POC); Black, Indigenous, and people of color (BIPOC), which acknowledges that Black and Indigenous people experience different and often deeper and more historical racism and discrimination than people of color from other racial backgrounds;[6] non-white; none of those terms? There is no right answer to this question because people are not monoliths. The population at focus of this book are people who have mental illness and who are outside of the social system default. I use the

5. The great American novelist Toni Morrison once said, "In this country American means white. Everybody else has to hyphenate." The Guardian, Jan. 29, 1992.

6. *BIPOC, Merriam-Webster's Unabridged Dictionary*, https://www.merriam-webster.com/dictionary/BIPOC (last visited Mar. 27, 2022).

term "people of diverse backgrounds" when recalling this focus to draw attention to, as described earlier, the complex intersectional identities that can expand beyond race, ethnicity, and culture and that influence the challenges and inequities faced by people moving through the criminal justice system and moving through social systems.

There are occasions when the book names specific racial demographics or characteristics. This is intentional. They describe specific subgroups or classifications specified in research. Terms used in these occasions are not interchangeable with any other terms.

"Behavioral health" when described in the context of this book describes the needs and conditions addressed through public health and social service systems. Behavioral health can include mental illness, substance use disorders, traumatic brain injury, and intellectual or developmental disability. "Mental illness" refers to conditions defined in the *Diagnostic and Statistical Manual of Mental Disorders* (DSM) or defined as mental health conditions in state or federal statutes. Other behavioral health conditions used in the book are defined in the context in which they appear. "Social determinants of mental health" refer to biological, social, and environmental factors that can influence mental health and the progression of mental illness. Social determinates encompass race, ethnicity, gender assigned at birth, gender identity, age, income level, education level, sexual orientation, geographic location, housing status, community dynamics, and family dynamics.[7]

I define terms articulating equity and race through the following meanings. "Racial disparity" refers to the unequal treatment or outcomes for different racial or ethnic groups in the same circumstance or at the same decision point when compared to the overall population. "Disparity" refers to differences not resulting from actual variations in clinical need or preferences. These are differences caused by structural barriers and subjective factors (e.g., biases, stereotyping, clinical uncertainty) that result in the differential treatment of people of diverse backgrounds. "Structural barriers" refer to barriers common among people

7. *Social Determinants*, U.S. Department of Health and Human Services, Office of Disease Prevention and Health Promotion, https://www.healthypeople.gov/2020/leading-health-indicators/2020-lhitopics/Mental health/determinants (last accessed Apr. 22, 2020).

and communities that are traditionally marginalized, such as low socioeconomic levels, over-policing, and low access to health care. "Racial disproportionality" refers to the ratio between the percentage of people in a particular racial or ethnic group at a particular decision point or when experiencing an event compared to the percentage of the same racial or ethnic group in the overall population (e.g., Black adults made up 33 percent of the U.S. prison population in 2017 despite Black adults representing only 12 percent of the U.S. adult population[8]). This ratio could suggest underrepresentation, proportional representation, or overrepresentation. It is incorrect to use racial disparity and racial disproportionality interchangeably. Racial disproportionality indicates a more specific problem than racial disparity.

"Equity" refers to the fair treatment of all people by considering individual needs and differences, such as gaps in opportunity and discrimination. It is incorrect to use "equity" interchangeably with "equality" or "parity." "Structural inequities" refer to the systemic disadvantage of one social group compared to other groups with whom they coexist. The term encompasses structural inequities in policy, law, governance, and culture. "Historical inequities" refer to systemic inequities that are rooted in past or early social systems. Historical inequities influence current unfair differences, regardless of the current presence or absence of inequity.

Structural Design of This Book and Its Chapters

This book will assist attorneys in first developing a foundational understanding of the prevalence of mental illness and racial inequity in the criminal justice system. It will then provide key concepts necessary for attorneys to develop their own personal equity framework and approaches to their legal practice. The book will also focus on providing attorneys with equity tools that can be immediately used within their practice.

The chapters of this book are grouped into five sections. Part I provides an overview of the problems facing the criminal justice system—the

---

8. John Gramlich, *The gap between the number of blacks and whites in prison is shrinking*, Pew Research Center (Apr. 30, 2019), https://www.pewresearch.org/fact-tank/2019/04/30/shrinking-gap-between-number-of-blacks-and-whites-in-prison/.

system disproportionately impacts people of diverse backgrounds who have mental illness and underserves them through the legal process. It then provides a foundational overview of mental illness and stigma, and indicators for identifying them within the context of the attorney role. Part II studies cultural awareness and cultural competency through a mental health and justice lens. It later details strategies for adopting tools and best practices for improving interactions between criminal justice professionals and people who become involved in the criminal cases. Part III dissects the roles of prosecutors and defense attorneys to explore role-specific opportunities to intervene and advance equity at distinct stages of a case. Part IV takes an in-depth look at the criminal justice continuum—from initial criminal justice involvement through post-adjudication and the aftermath of justice involvement—to highlight areas where criminal justice professionals can evoke change. Part V addresses the unique challenges that witnesses, victims, and survivors of crime face and provides specific tools for engaging them through the legal process. Part VI shifts focus to governing authorities and administrative processes and highlights techniques to move from theory to action while creating measurable change. The book concludes with an illustration of how the various concepts and tools can impact a real case and makes a call to action for attorneys to seek equity in the pursuit of justice.

This book is designed for every attorney who handles criminal cases, regardless of experience with cases involving people who have mental illness or with social justice topics. The concepts in the book are deep enough to provide new insights to those well-versed in topics covered, while simple enough that novices can walk away with immediately usable techniques and a conceptual framework for incorporating equitable lawyering into their practice. Finally, a list of tools and resources follows each chapter to support further learning and to address cases at hand. Following the theme of equity, all tools and resources listed are accessible to all attorneys, regardless of financial and resources availability.

PART I

Foundations

CHAPTER 1
Scoping the Problem

For most communities across the country, jails are the de facto mental health institutions.

Statements like this once shocked criminal justice professionals and the general public alike but are now commonplace in public discourse. National research supports this statement, finding that there are seven times more people who have mental illness in jails and prisons than there are in mental health treatment facilities.[1] In fact, more than half of all people housed in jails and prisons have a mental illness. Sixty-four percent of people in jails, 56 percent of people in state prisons, and 45 percent of people in federal prisons[2] have a mental illness compared to only 21 percent of people in the general public.[3] This disparity is even more staggering when one looks at serious mental illness among adults and at youth moving through the juvenile justice system. Roughly one in six adults in jail (or 17 percent) have a serious mental illness compared to

1. *Data-Driven Justice Playbook*, National Association of Counties, https://www.naco.org/resources/signature-projects/data-driven-justice (last visited Mar. 27, 2022).

2. Doris J. James & Lauren E. Glaze, Mental Health Problems of Prison and Jail Inmates 1 (Bureau of Justice Statistics Special Report, 2006).

3. *Mental Illness*, National Institute of Mental Health, https://www.nimh.nih.gov/health/statistics/mental-illness (last visited Mar. 27, 2022).

one in 20 adults in the general public (under 6 percent).[4] For youth moving through the justice system, roughly one in two youths (approximately 50 to 75 percent) meet criteria for a mental health disorder.[5]

The nexus between mental illness and criminal justice involvement is astounding. Poor mental health outcomes increase the likelihood of an individual becoming involved in the criminal justice system.[6] Once incarcerated, people who have mental illness tend to stay longer. They tend to have negative criminal justice outcomes that, in turn, lead to higher rates of recidivism after release.[7] These realities are especially evidenced among people of diverse backgrounds who experience avoidable and addressable inequities that are prevalent across mental health and criminal justice systems.[8] Attorneys must use their role to address these inequities. The role of the attorney is vital in achieving justice and disrupting the cycle of poor mental health outcomes and recidivism. To do this, attorneys must adopt an equitable approach for seeking access to justice.

Neither the criminal justice system nor legal process operates in a vacuum that is unaffected by social interactions and social inequities. Racial and health inequities impact the legal process, including inequities entrenched in the criminal justice system. Attorneys on both sides of the courtroom can play a role in combating inequities that impede justice

---

4. Henry Steadman et al., *Prevalence of Serious Mental Illness Among Jail Inmates*, 60 Psychiatric Serv. at 761 (2009); Ronald C. Kessler et al., *Prevalence, Severity, and Comorbidity of Twelve-month DSM-IV Disorders in the National Comorbidity Survey Replication (NCS-R)*, 64 Arch. Gen. Psychiatry at 618, 622 (2005); *Mental Illness*, National Institute of Mental Health, https://www.nimh.nih.gov/health/statistics/mental-illness (last visited Mar. 27, 2022).

5. Lee A. Underwood & Aryssa Washington, *Mental Illness and Juvenile Offenders*, 13 Int'l J. Env't Res. Pub. Health at 228 (2016).

6. David Cloud, *On Life Support: Public Health in the Age of Mass Incarceration*, Vera Institute of Justice (Nov. 2014), https://www.vera.org/publications/on-life-support-public-health-in-the-age-of-mass-incarceration.

7. Paula M. Ditton, Mental Health and Treatment of Inmates and Probationers (Bureau of Justice Statistics Special Report, 1999); *The Prevalence of Co-occurring Mental and Substance Use Disorders in Jails*, National GAINS Center for People with Co-Occurring Disorders in the Justice System (2004), https://taadas.s3.amazonaws.com/files/b4be5ac3283d2d751425d69a47f02357-The%20Prevalence%20of%20Co-Occurring%20Mental%20Illness%20and%20Substance%20Use%20Disorders%20in%20Jails.pdf.

8. *E.g.*, less access to mental health care, overrepresentation in the criminal justice system, and so on.

by advancing equity for people of diverse backgrounds who have mental illness. Adopting an equitable approach to the attorney role recognizes that people of diverse backgrounds who have mental illness experience discrimination, stigmatization, and reduced social opportunities that, when left unaddressed, prevent them from receiving full and fair access to justice.

Attorneys can adopt an equitable approach by considering individual needs and differences. These needs and differences can directly impact the case at hand and can impact the effectiveness of the legal process and ultimate criminal justice outcomes. To begin cultivating opportunities to advance equity, attorneys must understand the nexus between mental illness, race, and criminal justice involvement. This chapter provides a cursory overview of mental illness and its impact on people of diverse backgrounds. It then provides insight into the prevalence of people of diverse backgrounds who have mental illness in the criminal justice system and describes the barriers they face when moving through the system.

Defining the Nexus: Criminal Justice, Race, and Mental Illness

Mental illness is a broad term that covers numerous conditions and diagnoses. Mental illness varies in degree of severity, ranging on a spectrum from mild to moderate to severe or serious. For the nonclinically trained eye, mental illness is often associated with people who have serious mental illness. These are people who experience the most severe degree of symptoms, such as those evaluated for competence to stand trial before proceedings can move forward or those placed in civil conservatorships. Associating mental illness solely with serious mental illness can deflect away from people whose symptoms are less severe, leading to missed opportunities to provide effective legal responses.

There are key areas impacting the nexus of race, criminal justice involvement, and mental illness. Social determinants of mental health, intersectional identities, and racial inequity each play a role in the causal chain of criminal justice involvement. These contextual factors are interconnected, and they shape risk factors for criminal activity. It is important to review these factors to determine their influence on alleged criminal activity, criminal justice involvement, victimization, legal responses, and litigation tactics.

Social determinants of mental health are the social, environmental, and economic conditions that impact and affect mental health outcomes across populations. Social determinants include race and ethnicity, gender assigned at birth and gender identity, age, income level, educational attainment, geographic location, housing status, community dynamics, and family dynamics.[9] Determinants are shaped by social factors, such as policy and the distribution of power, money, and other resources at global, national, state, and local levels. Unmet mental illness and unaddressed social determinates of mental health create a pathway to criminal justice involvement.[10]

People's intersectional identities affect their lived experiences, including lived experiences shaped by social determinants of mental health. Intersectional identities[11] include race, gender identity, sexual orientation, ability or disability, and class status.[12] Intersectional identities inform the theory of intersectionality, which explores the complex ways that people's identities overlap and compound to shape their experiences and to shape systems of privilege, oppression, and/or discrimination relative to them.[13]

---

9. *Social Determinants*, U.S. Department of Health and Human Services, Office of Disease Prevention and Health Promotion, https://www.healthypeople.gov/2020/leading-health-indicators/2020-lhi-topics/Mental-Health (last accessed Apr. 22, 2020).

10. Anne Milgram et al., *Integrated Health Care and Criminal Justice Data—Viewing the Intersection of Public Safety, Public Health, and Public Policy Through a New Lens: Lessons from Camden, New Jersey*, Program in Criminal Justice Policy and Management, Harvard Kennedy School, at 16, 17 (2008).

11. Intersectional identities are social groupings. See *Chapter Two: Getting Grounded: Foundational Practice Tips for Recognizing Mental Illness and Stigma* for more detailed information about social groupings and their impact on people of diverse backgrounds who have mental illness.

12. Anne Sisson Runyan, *What Is Intersectionality and Why Is It Important? Building Solidarity in the Fight for Social Justice*, American Association of University Professors, https://www.aaup.org/article/what-intersectionality-and-why-it-important#.Yjolwk3MLHo (last visited Mar. 27, 2022).

13. *Intersectionality*, Merriam-Webster's Unabridged Dictionary, https://www.merriam-webster.com/dictionary/intersectionality (last visited Mar. 27, 2022); *see generally* Kimberlé Crenshaw, *Mapping the Margins: Intersectionality, Identity Politics, and Violence against Women of Color*, 43 Stanford L. Rev. 1244 (1991).

Intersectionality also hints to specific disproportionalities and disparities in criminal justice involvement and health inequities. Transgender people of color, for instance, have disproportionately high rates of health inequities and criminal justice involvement.[14]

Coined by the legal scholar Kimberlé Crenshaw during her tenure in race and gender studies,[15] intersectionality understands that people are necessarily situated within structures and systems, and that their position in those structures and systems is inherently based on their identities. Crenshaw suggests that people's identities are separate categories and that those qualitatively different identities are not "exclusive or separable."[16] Not seeing and responding to people's intersectional identities, Crenshaw articulated, "ultimately limits the opportunities for meaningful intervention."[17]

Supported by Crenshaw and other scholars studying intersectionality, the theory expands beyond race and gender studies and now considers various social groupings and identities and applies across fields of study.[18] Within the criminal justice context, intersectionality demonstrates the ways that intersectional identities factor into crime,[19] criminal justice processes and responses, and criminal justice outcomes. Put in the words of Professor Ruth D. Peterson, "[w]hen a society is organized along race/ethnic lines, we cannot assume that the source and responses to crime, or the application of criminal justice, are race neutral in their effects and consequences."[20]

---

14. Jaime M. Grant et al., *Injustice at Every Turn: A Report of the National Transgender Discrimination Survey*, National Center for Transgender Equality & National Gay and Lesbian Task Force, at 72–85, 158–71 (2011).

15. *See* Kimberlé Crenshaw, *Demarginalizing the Intersection of Race and Sex: A Black Feminist Critique of Antidiscrimination Doctrine, Feminist Theory and Antiracist Politics*, 1989 University of Chicago Legal Forum 139–67 (1989).

16. Crenshaw, *supra* note 13, at 1244.

17. *Id.* at 1251.

18. *Id.* at 1244, 1296; Devon W. Carbado et al., *Intersectionality: Mapping the Movements of a Theory*, 10 Du Bois Rev. 305 (2014).

19. Moving forward, this book uses the terms "intersectionality" and "intersectional identities" interchangeably.

20. Ruth D. Peterson, *Central Place of Race in Crime and Justice—The American Society of Criminology's 2011 Sutherland Address*, 50 Criminology 319 (2012).

The compounding discrimination intertwined in intersectional identities and social determinants of mental health are prominent drivers of health disparities and health inequities. People of diverse backgrounds experience more health disparities compered to white people.[21] Health disparities refer to the differences in health outcomes among distinct groups of people. People of diverse backgrounds also face greater health inequities than white people. Health inequities represent disparities in health that result from avoidable systemic and unfair social and economic policies and practices that create barriers to opportunity.[22] When people of diverse backgrounds do receive mental health treatment for instance, they are less likely to receive guidance-consistent care.[23] Additionally, experiencing racism contributes to health disparities and health inequities. Racism is a contributing factor to the onset and aggravation of mental illness.[24] People who experience racism have higher rates of mental illness than people who do not suffer those experiences. Racism itself also leads to inequities in access to health care.[25] This, in turn, leads to poorer health outcomes when compared to people who do not experience the harms of racism.[26]

Mental Illness and Treatment in the General Public

Before we explore the scope of people of diverse backgrounds who have mental illness within the criminal justice system, it is important to grasp the prevalence of mental illness across the general public. Recognizing

---

21. National Academies of Sciences et al., Committee on Community-Based Solutions to Promote Health Equity in the United States (James N. Weinstein et al. eds., 2017); Ruth S. Shimm & Sarah Y. Vinson, *Social (In)Justice and Mental Health*, *in* Social (In)justice and Mental Health, 3, 4–11 (Ruth S. Shim & Sarah Y. Vinson eds., 1st ed. 2021).

22. *See* National Academies of Sciences et al., *supra* note 21.

23. *Black/African American*, National Alliance on Mental Illness, https://nami.org/Your-Journey/Identity-and-Cultural-Dimensions/Black-African-American (last visited Mar. 27, 2022).

24. Yin Paradies et al., *Racism as a Determinant of Health: A Systematic Review and Meta-Analysis*, 10 PLoS ONE (2015).

25. *The Impact of Structural Racism on Mental Health*, Mental Health Technology Transfer Center Network, https://mhttcnetwork.org/sites/default/files/2021-04/MHTTC_StructuralRacism_Final.pdf (last visited Mar. 27, 2022).

26. Paradies, *supra* note 24.

mental illness and access to treatment in the general public provides a meaningful comparison to the gravity of mental illness and access to treatment for people of diverse backgrounds who become justice involved.

Adults who are Black, Indigenous, and People of Color (BIPOC) are just as likely as white adults to have mental illness (roughly 19 percent of BIPOC adults compared to 20 percent of white adults), but they are 45 percent less likely to receive needed treatment. Roughly one in two white adults receives treatment (about 48 percent), while 30 percent of BIPOC adults receive needed treatment.[27] Similar health inequities are reflected across serious mental illness. Serious mental illness presents great functional impairments across adults of all races. While BIPOC and white adults have roughly the same prevalence rates for serious mental illness (roughly 4.6 percent of BIPOC adults compared to 5 percent of white adults), white adults are 23 percent more likely than BIPOC adults to receive treatment. Roughly 71 percent of white adults who have a serious mental illness receive treatment, but only 56 percent of Black and Latine adults receive treatment.[28]

Race, Mental Illness, and Criminal Justice Involvement

People who have mental illness are overrepresented in the criminal justice system. Even with known data about this population, the actual number of people who have mental illness who are involved in the criminal justice system is modest, as many people go unidentified. There is limited data looking specifically at the intersection of race, criminal justice involvement, and mental illness. Though data on this intersection is growing in sophistication, it is important to avoid making piecemeal or antidotal assumptions by patching together data looking individually at race and mental illness prevalence among the criminal justice population. Doing this further skews the realities about who moving through the legal

27. National Institute of Mental Health, *supra* note 3.

28. *Id.* (There are no comparable statistics for Asian and Pacific Islander and Indigenous adults at the time of this writing.)

process is identified as having mental illness and who receives informed legal responses.

Criminal justice professionals, including attorneys, carry influence in determining who moving through the justice system is identified as having mental illness. The most common identification methods are screening and assessment during jail booking or through referral for a mental health evaluation. Mental health screens flag people who may have mental illness and recommend a full follow-up mental health evaluation to confirm results. Full evaluations allow mental health professionals to diagnose mental illness, decide on a treatment plan, and make recommendations to inform case disposition and sentencing decisions. There is a growing body of research examining how well this process identifies people who have mental illness, and the extent to which they access available court programs and other legal options. This research also highlights system shortcomings, particularly health disparities and health inequities for people of diverse backgrounds.

A best practice for reducing the length of avoidable time spent within the criminal justice system is to identify everyone who has a mental health need as early as possible. Identification can take place at any criminal justice access point, and identification often begins at jail booking. The most effective way to identify mental illness is through a universal screening process that screens everyone booked into jail using a standardized, validated screening tool. Many screening tools were developed to be conducted by nonclinical staff, such as correctional officers, and were designed to provide clear and consistent finding of who entering the jail has a mental health need and should be referred for a full diagnostic assessment.

Screening during the jail booking process is not the only way to identify people in the criminal justice system who have mental illness. For starters, most jurisdictions do not have a universal screening process in place, causing many people who have mental illness to fall through the identification gap. Jurisdictions that do incorporate screening during jail booking may also fail to capture accurate results. Many mental health screening tools were not controlled for race when undergoing validation studies and have since been determined to perpetuate inequities by falsely identifying people of diverse backgrounds as not having mental illness.[29] This means that identification of mental illness often falls on the shoulders of criminal justice professionals who make referrals for mental health evaluations.

People of diverse backgrounds are more likely to be underdiagnosed for mental illness while moving through the criminal justice system compared to white people. Data looking at mental health referrals comparing Black adults to non-Black adults shows that Black adults are 44 percent less likely to be referred for a mental health evaluation than their counterparts.[30] People of diverse backgrounds are also more likely to be misdiagnosed, incorrectly not diagnosed when they should have been, and incorrectly not referred for a mental health evaluation despite exhibiting behavior indicative of mental illness.[31] This is often due to the implicit and explicit assumptions of criminal justice professionals, including attorneys, who are responsible for making mental health evaluation referrals. Subjective assumptions that can influence referrals include biases, misunderstandings of socioeconomic and cultural differences, and other implicit or explicit assumptions. One common assumption is that people of diverse backgrounds are inherently criminal. When people of diverse backgrounds are exhibiting behaviors indicative of mental illness, criminal justice professionals and attorneys often assume they are acting suspicious and like a "criminal" rather than as having a mental health need.[32]

---

29. Seth J. Prins et al., *Exploring Racial Disparities in the Brief Jail Mental Health Screen*, 39 Crim. Just. & Behav. at 635–45 (2012).

30. Melissa Thompson, *Race, Gender, and the Social Construction of Mental Illness in the Criminal Justice System*, 53 Soc. Persp. at 99–126 (2010).

31. Melissa Thompson, Mad or Bad? Race, Class, Gender and Mental Disorder in the Criminal Justice System (LFB Scholarly Publishing, LLC 2010); Thomas G. McGuire & Jeanne Miranda, *New Evidence Regarding Racial and Ethnic Disparities in Mental Health: Policy Implications*, 27 Health Aff. at 393–403 (2008); U.S. Dep't of Health and Human Ser., Agency for Healthcare Research and Quality, AHRQ Pub. No. 16-0015, 2015 National Healthcare Quality and Disparities Report and 5th Anniversary Update on the National Quality Strategy 6–7 (2016).

32. Thompson, *supra* note 31.

Mental Health Treatment in the Criminal Justice System

People of diverse backgrounds are less likely than white people to receive mental health treatment when incarcerated. Black adults receive significantly less mental health treatment while in correctional settings than their non-Black counterparts.[33] These statistics are reflected for people who have a history of mental illness prior to incarceration and for people who were recently diagnosed.[34] Black adults are also significantly less likely to receive psychiatric medication and counseling while in prison than their non-Black counterparts. This means that Black adults in prison are more likely than non-Black adults to be hospitalized even though treatment may be more appropriately provided outside of the hospital setting.[35] This trend extends to mental health treatment provided in any situation involving criminal justice professionals. Take connections to care made by law enforcement and emergency personnel who respond to calls for service. Compared to white adults, law enforcement and emergency personnel are more likely to refer Black and Latine adults to involuntary inpatient hospitalization rather than to lesser restrictive community-based care.[36]

Looking beyond adults, this disparity burdens youth moving through the juvenile justice system. Research shows that youth of color who have behavioral health needs are more likely than white youth to be referred to the juvenile justice system rather than the health care systems.[37] White youth are significantly more likely to be diagnosed with mental illness while only a small portion of Black youth are referred for mental health services.[38] In explorations of the cause of these disparities, race and eth-

---

33. Thompson, *supra* note 31.
34. *Id.*
35. *Id.*
36. Julian Chun-Chung Chow et al., *Racial/Ethnic Disparities in the Use of Mental Health Services in Poverty Areas*, 93 Am. J. Pub. Health 792–97 (2003).
37. Henna Budhwani et al., *Depression in Racial and Ethnic Minorities: The Impact of Nativity and Discrimination*, 2 Racial Ethnic Health Disparities at 34–42 (2015).
38. Anne Dannerbeck Janku & Jiahui Yan, *Exploring Patterns of Court-Ordered Mental Health Services for Juvenile Offenders: Is There Evidence of Systemic Bias?*, 36 Crim. Just. & Behav. at 402–19 (2009).

nicity were shown to be the most influential predictive factors in determining whether youth would be sent through the mental health system or the juvenile justice system. Race and ethnicity were greater factors than actual psychological or psychosocial needs.[39]

Disparities in mental health treatment are contrary to the least-restrictive alternative principle used when determining the course of behavioral health treatment. The least-restrictive alternative principle advocates for government systems to connect people to treatment while preserving as much of their freedom as can be safely done by safeguarding against unnecessary infringement of individual rights.[40] Derived from *Shelton v. Tucker*, 364 U.S. 479 (1960), "even though the governmental purpose be legitimate and substantial, that purpose cannot be pursued by means that broadly stifle fundamental personal liberties when the end can be more narrowly achieved." State law or local policy interprets this principle to encourage treatment that is least disruptive to usual routines. Criminal justice strategies embrace the least-restrictive alternative principle by recognizing that people who have mental illness can be appropriately served through mental health systems instead of criminal justice systems. When incarceration is unavoidable, the strategies strengthen the continuum of mental health care during incarceration and upon release from jail or prison. The strategies, however, can be effective only if they are available to and accessed by everyone who can benefit from them.

Opportunities for Attorney Intervention

The prevalence of mental illness is relatively uniform across people of all races, yet people of diverse backgrounds are less likely than white people to receive mental health treatment in the community or in jail and prison settings. Access to treatment in the community seems to be a key driver in identifying who within the criminal justice system has mental illness, but people of diverse backgrounds often lack adequate access to

---

39. Floyd Westendorp et al., *Variables which Differentiate Placement of Adolescents into Juvenile Justice or Mental Health Systems*, 21 ADOLESCENCE at 23–37 (1986).
40. J.M. Johnston & Robert A. Sherman, *Applying the Least Restrictive Alternative Principle to Treatment Decisions: A Legal and Behavioral Analysis*, 16 THE BEHAV. ANALYST at 103–15 (1993).

such treatment. Referrals for mental health evaluations also drive access to mental health treatment, but referrals are often subject to the assumptions and cultural misconceptions of the criminal justice professionals who are in charge of making them. As dismal as these takeaways may be, they establish a starting point for attorneys to discover opportunities to effectively use their position to advance equity and fairness. Attorneys can begin doing this by identifying opportunities ripe for intervention and developing responsive lawyering skills.

Tools and Resources

- *Mental Health Facts in Brief: Relevance of Social Determinants in Mental Health* by the National Judicial Task Force to Examine State Courts' Response to Mental Illness.
- Kimberlé Crenshaw, *Mapping the Margins: Intersectionality, Identity Politics, and Violence against Women of Color*, 43 STANFORD L. REV. 1241–99 (1991).

CHAPTER 2

Getting Grounded: Foundational Practice Tips for Recognizing Mental Illness and Stigma

More than two million people who have mental illness are booked into jails each year.[1] While jails and other criminal justice decision points are becoming more sophisticated in identifying when people have mental illness, many people go without their mental illness being identified. Even if identified, mental health needs often remain unmet. People of diverse backgrounds who have mental illness are more likely than white people to end up in jail or prison.[2] Once incarcerated, they are less likely to

1. *Decriminalizing Mental Illness*, National Alliance on Mental Illness, https://www.nami.org/getattachment/Get-Involved/NAMI-National-Convention/Convention-Program-Schedule/Hill-Day-2017/FINAL-Hill-Day-17-Leave-Behind-_De-Criminalizing-Mental-Illness.pdf (last visited Mar. 27, 2022)

2. Leah Pope, *Racial Disparities in Mental Health and Criminal Justice*, National Alliance on Mental Illness, https://www.nami.org/Blogs/NAMI-Blog/July-2019/Racial-Disparities-in-Mental-Health-and-Criminal-Justice (Jul. 2019).

have their mental illness acknowledged and addressed.[3] The prevalence of these health inequities in the criminal justice system suggests that it is not a matter of if attorneys will come across cases involving people of diverse backgrounds who have mental illness. It is a matter of when.

Most attorneys understand the ethical obligations and challenges that can arise when they handle cases involving people who have mental illness. There may be specific procedural options or requirements depending on the severity of the mental illness. There may be opportunities to access prosecutor-led or court diversion. Due process determinations may allow for mental health treatment while charges are pending. Court proceedings may be paused due to reduced or diminished capacity or inability to assist with one's own defense. While the nature of each case and the needs arising out of mental illness vary, attorneys should understand mental illness and how it converges with race and culture to determine when legal intervention is appropriate.

Recognizing Mental Illness: A Primer for Lawyers

Mental illness is a mental, behavioral, or emotional disorder that impacts every person who has it differently. Mental illness can range in severity from no impairment to mild or moderate impairment to severe or serious impairment.[4] The burden of the layman's understanding of mental illness falls on serious mental illness, and mental illness is conventionally interpreted through a default and binary lens.

Mental illness is characterized by the diagnosis of a specific condition or disorder, the duration of symptoms, and the degree of functional impairment. Functional impairment assesses the ability to comply with

---

3. Melissa Thompson, *Gender, Race, and Mental Illness in the Criminal Justice System*, 1 Corr. & Mental Health An Update of the Nat'l Inst. of Corr., no. 1, 2011, at 4.

4. *Mental Illness*, National Institute of Mental Health, https://www.nimh.nih.gov/health/statistics/mental-illness (last visited Mar. 27, 2022) [hereinafter National Institute of Mental Health].

rules, adhere to routines, and maintain basic hygiene.[5] People meeting the criteria for serious mental illness are generally used to illustrate the entire spectrum of mental illness despite being a subset of mental illness severity. Serious mental illness is often recognizable even to untrained eyes, and mental illness reaching this level indicates significant treatment needs. Serious mental illness is also widely used nomenclature to connote legal terminology. The term is defined in federal and state statutes to prioritize publicly funded mental health treatment and other governmental priorities.

Recognizing mental illness includes recognizing mental illness across levels of severity and recognizing the impact that race and culture can have on it. Race and culture can influence ideals around acknowledging and treating mental illness, and they can shape how people, communities, and mental health systems respond. Culture can also denote stigma of mental illness. Mental health systems can also carry stigma of race or culture, and of criminal justice involvement. Cultural differences between people who have mental illness and mental health professionals can lead to unmet mental health needs. An example of this is where culture influences the way people interpret their mental illness and describe their symptoms. When mental health professionals are unfamiliar with cultural influences, they may disregard or misinterpret cultural expressions of mental illness. Cultural disconnect heightens the risk of misdiagnoses.[6] Misdiagnoses may involve over- or underdiagnosing the severity of a mental illness, making incorrect diagnosis determinations, or incorrectly determining the absence of a mental illness.

Attorneys on both sides of the courtroom can advocate for people who become involved in the criminal justice system to ensure they are appropriately evaluated for mental illness. By learning basic signs and symptoms of a mental illness, including culturally informed signs, attorneys can use their professional judgment to call for mental health evaluations or second opinions.

---

5. *Id.*

6. Office of the Surgeon General et al., Mental Health: Culture, Race, and Ethnicity: A Supplement to Mental Health: A Report of the Surgeon General (2001), https://www.ncbi.nlm.nih.gov/books/NBK44249/ (last visited Mar. 27, 2022).

Mental Illness verses Behavioral Health

Behavioral health is a blanket term that includes mental health and, in turn, mental illness. Behavioral health also encompasses conditions that can carry the same symptoms of mental illness and that are common among people involved in the criminal justice system. The term "behavioral health" as it concerns the criminal justice system connotes legal terminology defined in federal and state statute that is often used to set parameters around federal funding and other public health priorities. Behavioral health conditions in the statutory sense may embody intellectual or developmental disorders (also known as I/DD), substance use (casual use that is not as severe as addiction), substance use disorder (a diagnosed addiction, also known as SUD), traumatic brain injury (also known as TBI), fetal alcohol syndrome, and neurodivergence (e.g., autism or attention deficit hyperactivity disorder). Although some of these disorders may have the same effect on behavior as mental illness, they are treated differently in terms of both medical treatment and, in most jurisdictions, statutory authority governing available criminal justice and legal remedies.

Behavioral health conditions can co-occur, and the appearance of multiple behavioral health conditions can be expressed simultaneously. Mental illness can be exhibited differently in people who have co-occurring conditions. Co-occurring conditions include mental illness that co-occurs with a substance use disorder, intellectual or developmental disability, traumatic brain injury, or other physical or behavioral health conditions. The term is commonly used by criminal justice professionals to denote co-occurring mental illness and substance use disorders.[7] Mental illness when impacted by substance use may present differently or identically depending on the circumstances. Mental illness that co-occurs

7. *Substance Use and Co-Occurring Mental Disorders*, National Institute of Mental Health, https://www.nimh.nih.gov/health/topics/substance-use-and-mental-health (last visited Mar. 27, 2022).

with substance use disorders, for instance, may receive a different prognosis and medical response than substance-induced psychoses.[8]

Mental illness can also impact people of certain ages differently. Juveniles and transition-aged youth, whose brains are not yet fully developed, experience mental illness and are diagnosed differently than adults. Geriatric populations may have changes in existing mental illness or have mental illness onset during the aging process.[9] Attorneys need not become experts in differentiating mental illness from other behavioral health conditions or by variations across age groups, but they should become familiar with certain behavioral indicators that can raise the need for a mental health evaluation.

Indicators in Speech Patterns[10]

Mental illness can be noticeable through speech. Mental illness can cause speech to be rapid, slow, or slurred. People may experience speech language difficulties. This may be difficulty recalling or finding words, or frequently skipping words. Mental illness may cause unusually long delays or pauses, unusually short or long answers, or stutters. People may speak incoherently, use a made-up language, or speak nonsensically.

Speech pattern indicators can also be attributed to other behavioral health conditions. This can include speech, language, and swallowing difficulties; head injury and traumatic brain injury; substance use; or substance use disorders. Some speech patterns may also result from cultural

---

8. Substance Abuse and Mental Health Services Administration, *Substance Use Disorder Treatment for People with Co-Occurring Disorders Treatment Improvement Protocol 42*, 122 (2020), https://store.samhsa.gov/sites/default/files/SAMHSA_Digital_Download/PEP20-02-01-004_Final_508.pdf (last visited Mar. 27, 2022).

9. Ronald Kessler et al., *Age of Onset of Mental Disorders: A Review of Recent Literature*, 20 Current Opinion in Psychiatry, no. 4, 2007, 359–64; Brie A. Williams et al., *Addressing the Aging Crisis in U.S. Criminal Justice Health Care*, 60 J. Am. Geriatric Soc'y, no. 6, 2012, 1150–56; National Institute of Mental Health, *supra* note 4.

10. Unless otherwise cited, the sources for information in this section are from Diagnostic and Statistical Manual of Mental Disorders (Am. Psychiatric Assoc. 5th ed, 2013) [hereinafter DSM]; *Mental Health Medications*, National Institute of Mental Health, https://www.nimh.nih.gov/health/topics/mental-health-medications (last visited Mar. 27, 2022).

influences and upbrings. The speed of speech or the use of certain dialect, for instance, may be specific to a community or social group.

Indicators in Thought Patterns[11]

Symptoms of mental illness can be reflected through thought patterns. Mental illness can impact cognition. This can be manifested through confusion, gaps in memory, disorientation, lack of insight into one's behaviors, difficulty picking up on social cues, difficulty complying with instructions, or loss of time. Thought pattern interruptions can be displayed through unusual ideas or disorganized thoughts. This may be displayed as circular or tangential thought, hyperfixation on certain facts, belief in having special powers, and paranoia. People may have thoughts or experiences that others present do not have. Mental illness may cause people to express conflicting or extreme emotions and reactions, or cause distractibility. Delusions, including visual and auditory hallucinations and irrational fears, may be exhibited. This can be observed as responses to internal voices or stimuli, or detachment from reality.

Symptoms impacting thought pattern may extend beyond mental illness and be a sign of other behavioral health conditions. This can include symptoms expressed due to high levels of anxiety or symptoms resulting from substance use.

Indicators in Body Language[12]

Symptoms of mental illness may be observed through body language. People may appear catatonic, as expressed through vacant stares, unusual facial expressions, not speaking, not responding to surroundings or stimuli, repetitive movements, and agitation. Mental illness can cause people to be tense, hypervigilant, excessively uncooperative, belligerent, disrespectful, unusually inattentive, or to act without regard for the situation. Mental illness can be reflected through subtle body language. People may avoid making eye contact, experience increased clumsiness,

11. *Id.*
12. *Id.*

appear indifferent or morose, experience slowed or delayed movements or speech, or present disjoined emotions.

Body language can be impacted by other triggers, including side effects of medication, trauma responses, or other behavioral health conditions. Some benign behaviors may result from cultural influences and community traumas. Not making eye contact with authority figures may be reflective of cultural norms or experience-based mistrust.[13] Hyperarousal, or hypervigilance, may result from trauma and experience-based mistrust.[14] This can cause people to appear tense or anxious, or to be in "fight or flight" mode.

Indicators in Physical Symptoms[15]

Mental illness can trigger physical symptoms, both unobservable symptoms that are experienced internally and symptoms that can be visible to others. Unobservable symptoms can include sleep disorders such as insomnia or hypersomnia, headaches, dizziness, aches, pains, and gastrointestinal disorders. Visible symptoms can include mobility issues, rapid eye blinking, tremors, and other uncontrollable body movements. People may appear older or younger than their biological age, be dressed inappropriately for weather conditions, lose control of bodily functions, or have observable bruises or wounds resulting from self-harm or unusual clumsiness.

Physical symptoms may be unrelated to mental illness and caused by other behavioral health conditions. Physical behaviors can be triggered by intellectual or developmental disorders, traumatic brain injury, substance use, and other conditions can be mistaken for mental illness. Physical symptoms can also be a side effect of medication.

---

13. Substance Abuse and Mental Health Services Administration, Improving Cultural Competence Treatment Improvement Protocol 59 (2014), https://www.ncbi.nlm.nih.gov/books/NBK248431 (last visited Mar. 27, 2022).
14. Substance Abuse and Mental Health Services Administration, Trauma-Informed Care in Behavioral Health Services Treatment Improvement Protocol 57 (2014), https://www.ncbi.nlm.nih.gov/books/NBK207191 (last visited Mar. 27, 2022).
15. DSM, *supra* note 10.

Indicators in Lexicon and Local Lingo

People who have received previous treatment for mental illness may have advanced knowledge of mental health terms. This can include knowing the names and terms of diagnoses, medications, treatment modalities, local mental health or hospital facilities, case workers or clinicians, and other terms specific to mental health treatment and the local environment.

Discovering Mental Illness through Collateral Sources

Some people may know of their mental illness, be it through awareness of their symptoms or through previous diagnoses. Others may not know or believe that they have mental illness or believe that their condition no longer requires treatment or management. People may also hide their mental illness. This may be done out of fear of negative repercussions when housed in jail or prison, fear or receiving negative disposition outcomes, or fear or distrust of medical staff, law enforcement, attorneys, and other criminal justice professionals. Attorneys may receive mental health information through investigation or collateral sources even if people do not provide that information themselves. Attorneys should avoid surprising people with information obtained through collateral sources and avoid insinuating that people who withhold mental health information are doing so for dishonest reasons.

Self-disclosure of mental health conditions is associated with perceptions of safety and nonjudgment.[16] Failure to disclose mental illness may result from experience-based mistrust of attorneys or of the criminal justice system. Attorneys can build trust by moving away from a legal approach and adopting a relational approach.[17] In addition to building trust, this approach promotes a sense of procedural justice. Procedural justice is the perception that people are treated fairly when

16. Substance Abuse and Mental Health Services Administration, Self-Disclosure and Its Impact on Individuals Who Receive Mental Health Services (2008).

17. *See, e.g.*, Jill Howieson & Shane L. Rogers, *Rethinking the Lawyer-Client Interview: Taking a Relational Approach*, 26 Psychiatry Psych. & L., no. 4, 2019, 659–68.

moving through the legal system. Procedural justice looks at the process that people experience when moving through the justice system, rather than focusing on people's perception of the outcome of their case. When people believe they are being treated fairly, they are more likely to express positive behavioral change, have higher levels of respect and satisfaction with attorneys, and be more willing to comply with legal processes and court mandates.[18] Once trust is established, attorneys can pursue questions that will allow people to be open about their mental illness or symptoms indicative of a mental health need.

Failure to disclose mental illness can also be rooted in the mental illness itself.[19] This can be addressed by building on the relational approach by asking open-ended questions to get people to discuss their mental health history or their symptoms. Springing information found through collateral sources on them may damage trust and may trigger mental illness systems. People who suffer paranoia, for instance, may be triggered if attorneys recite mental health information that they had not disclosed themselves.

In either case, explain any impact that hiding important mental health information may have on the case. Depending on their role, attorneys may approach mental health histories differently. Prosecutors should avoid using mental health information as a litigation tactic. Only disclose information if doing so would lead to positive justice outcomes. Prosecutors should avoid using mental illness and mental health histories to establish punitive consequences. Defense attorneys should explain that hiding information may inhibit the attorneys' ability to effectively represent and advocate for them.

---

18. American Judges Association et al., Bench Card on Procedural Fairness Practical Tips for Courtroom Proceedings, https://www.judges.org/wp-content/uploads/2020/03/Procedural_Fairness_Bench_Card.pdf (last visited Mar. 27, 2022); Fair & Just Prosecution, Building Community Trust Procedural Justice: Enhancing the Legitimacy of the Justice System, https://www.fairandjustprosecution.org/staging/wp-content/uploads/2017/09/FJPBrief.ProceduralJustice.9.25.pdf (last visited Mar. 27, 2022).

19. *Anosognosia*, National Alliance on Mental Illness, https://www.nami.org/About-Mental-Illness/Common-with-Mental-Illness/Anosognosia#:~:text=The%20formal%20medical%20term%20for%20this%20medical%20condition,or%20that%20they%20can%E2%80%99t%20perceive%20their%20condition%20accurately (last visited Mar. 27, 2022).

Recognizing mental illness through observation or through collateral sources is the first step for attorneys to adapt their approaches to ensure cases are met with informed objectivity, fairness, and equity. The presence of mental illness is not the only factor that can impede justice for people of diverse backgrounds. Attorneys should become grounded in concepts tied to mental illness that can impact the legal process. Going hand-in-hand with recognizing mental illness is recognizing the stigma attached to it. Stigma of mental illness leads to the tendency to pathologize people who have it. Stigma of mental illness is more profound for people of diverse backgrounds[20] and can lead to negative legal consequences when they become involved in the criminal justice system.

Recognizing and Confronting Stigma

Mental illness and criminal justice involvement individually carry heavy stigmas. Combined, these stigmas are more profound for people of diverse backgrounds.[21] Stigma and pathologizing mental illness can discourage engagement and, oftentimes, reinforce silence.[22]

Stigmas are attributes rooted in negative and unfair stereotypes. Stigmas are magnified for people who identify as male, transgender, nonbinary, or genderqueer, and are magnified for people of diverse backgrounds.[23] Attorneys have a duty to identify and mitigate stigmas that may impact cases, including stigmas carried by the attorney, other

---

20. *See Mental Health Disparities: Diverse Populations*, American Psychiatric Association, https://www.psychiatry.org/psychiatrists/cultural-competency/education/mental-health-facts (last visited Mar. 27, 2022); Ozlem Eylem et al., *Stigma for Common Mental Disorders in Racial Minorities and Majorities: A Systematic Review and Meta-Analysis*, 20 BMC Pub. Health, no. 1, 2020.

21. Eylem, *supra* note 20.

22. Laura Prescott, *Defining the Role of Consumer-Survivors, in Trauma-Informed Systems, in* 89 Using Trauma Theory to Design Service Symptoms 83, 84 (Maxine Harris & Roger D. Fallot eds., 2001).

23. *Mental Health Disparities: Diverse Populations*, American Psychiatric Association, https://www.psychiatry.org/psychiatrists/cultural-competency/education/mental-health-facts (last visited Mar. 27, 2022); Center for American Progress et al., *Unjust: How the Broken Criminal Justice System Fails LGBT People of Color* 24 (2016), https://www.lgbtmap.org/file/lgbt-criminal-justice-poc.pdf (last visited Mar. 27, 2022).

criminal justice professionals, jurors, or other decision-makers. To do this, attorneys should be familiar with the basic concepts and consequences of stigma.

Core Concepts of Stigma

Stigma is a discrediting attribute applied to people or groups, such as a devalued social identity.[24] Stigma leads to stigmatization, the devaluation of people or groups through use of negative labels or stereotypes. Stigmatization is a social action that usually happens in the context of social groups or communities. Labels are terms that describe or define institutions, people, or experienced conditions. Labels are accepted by social groups or communities. Stereotypes are negative and unfair beliefs given to institutions, people, or experienced conditions. Embedded in stereotypes are prejudices, which are negative beliefs and attitudes. Stigmas, labels, and stereotypes lead to negative actions, including discrimination. Discrimination is prejudicial treatment endorsed or reinforced by stereotypes. Discrimination is performed by people, social groups, or communities.[25]

The characteristics of stigma can be described as either discredited or discreditable. A discredited stigma is an attribute that is easily discernable. A discredited stigma can be a physical attribute or social identity.[26] Physical attributes are body characteristics or bodily conditions, such as body shape or a physical disability.[27] Social identities are attributes that indicate which social group or social groups a person fits into and can be easily and initially perceived. Race is a social identity.[28] A discreditable

24. Erving Goffman, Stigma: Notes on the Management of Spoiled Identity (Touchstone 1963) [hereinafter Goffman]. *See also Stigma*, APA Dictionary of Psychology, https://dictionary.apa.org/stigma (last visited Mar. 27, 2022); Bernice A. Pescosolido & Jack K. Martin, *The Stigma Complex*, 41 Ann. Rev. of Socio., no. 1, 2015, 87–116 [hereinafter Pescosolido].

25. *See Pescosolido*, *supra* note 24.

26. Goffman, *supra* note 24.

27. *Pescosolido*, *supra* note 24.

28. Diane M. Quinn & Valerie A. Earnshaw, *Concealable Stigmatized Identities and Psychological Well-Being*, 7 Soc. & Personality Psych. Compass, no. 1, 2013, 40–51.

stigma is an attribute that is not immediately known or that is hidden.[29] It can include attributes such as social status. Social status is a position in society that is typically not immediately perceived based on social identities, such as wealth or educational attainment. A discreditable stigma can include stigma of character. Stigma of character are distinctive mental or moral qualities that are construed negatively. Mental and moral qualities include having a mental illness or having a criminal conviction.[30]

Stigmas can come in different forms. Courtesy stigma is stigma that extends to people who are associated with or close to stigmatized groups or stigmatized people. Practitioner stigma occurs when practitioners or professionals discriminate, prejudice, or stereotype stigmatized people or groups. Practitioner stigma is exercised overtly or covertly by practitioners who are designated to assist or interact with stigmatized people or groups in a professional setting.[31] This can be seen, for example, in racial profiling in stop and frisk policing.[32] Public stigma is discrimination, prejudices, and stereotypes that are socially accepted or endorsed by the general population.[33]

Stigmatization of any form can lead to self-stigma. Self-stigma occurs when people who are stigmatized internalize and self-accept the stereotypes assigned to them. Stigma can also happen on a structural level. Structural (or institutional) stigma occurs when discrimination, prejudices, and stereotypes are accepted, endorsed, or enacted by laws, policies, or institutions.[34] An illustration of this is war on drugs policies, which

---

29. Goffman, *supra* note 24.

30. *Id.*

31. *Pescosolido, supra* note 24.

32. *See, e.g.*, Floyd v. City of New York, 959 F. Supp. 2d 540 (S.D.N.Y. 2013).

33. *Pescosolido, supra* note 24. *See also Stigma, Prejudice and Discrimination Against People with Mental Illness*, American Psychiatric Association, https://www.psychiatry.org/patients-families/stigma-and-discrimination (last visited Mar. 27, 2022).

34. *Pescosolido, supra* note 24. *See also Stigma, Prejudice and Discrimination Against People with Mental Illness*, American Psychiatric Association, https://www.psychiatry.org/patients-families/stigma-and-discrimination (last visited Mar. 27, 2022).

disproportionately impact people of diverse backgrounds and diverse communities.[35]

Stigmas can be expressed and experienced differently, and stigma may be compounded. Anticipated stigma occurs when the people who are stigmatized expect to experience prejudice or discrimination.[36] This is shown when people of diverse backgrounds who have mental illness expect to be arrested when interacting with law enforcement instead of being connected to mental health urgent care centers. Enacted stigma occurs when discrimination against stigmatized people takes place.[37] Enacted stigma can be seen, for instance, when prosecutors intentionally up-charge people of diverse backgrounds who have mental illness when lesser charges and criminal justice penalties are appropriate. Endorsed stigmas are actions, inactions, and passivity that support, accept, or condone stereotypes, prejudice, or discrimination.[38] An example is not intervening when stigma influences case disposition despite opportunities for attorney intervention.

Stigma expressions and experiences can be perceived or received. Perceived stigmas are beliefs that devalue or discriminate against stigmatized people or groups. Perceived stigmas are socially accepted or would be socially accepted.[39] An example of perceived stigmas is the assumption that people of diverse backgrounds who have mental illness are acting unusual because they are inherently criminal rather than that they are experiencing symptoms of their mental illness. Received stigmas focus on the people experiencing stigmatization. Received stigma is rejecting or devaluing the discrimination or negative experiences that people

---

35. David Rudovsky, *The Impact of the War on Drugs on Procedural Fairness and Racial Equality*, 1994 Univ. of Chicago Legal F., no. 1, 1994. *See also* Lisa D. Moore & Amy Elkavich, *Who's Using and Who's Doing Time: Incarceration, the War on Drugs, and Public Health*, 98 Am. J. of Pub. Health, no. 5, 2008, 782–86.
36. *Pescosolido*, *supra* note 24.
37. *Id.*
38. *Id.*
39. Kelly E. Moore et al., *The Effect of Stigma on Criminal Offenders' Functioning: A Longitudinal Mediational Model*, 37 Deviant Behav., no. 2, 2016, 196–218.

or groups face.[40] This can be demonstrated when people participating in alternatives to incarceration state that they are not receiving culturally appropriate treatment but are ignored and instead assumed to be uncooperative.

Combating Stigma

Stigma within the criminal justice system and held by criminal justice professionals can arise in many situations. People of diverse backgrounds who have mental illness are especially prone to stigma based on their racial identity and mental illness. They may experience additional stigma that their intersectional identities carry. Once involved in the criminal justice system, enacted stigma may jeopardize the outcome of their case. Even as survivors of crime or witnesses, they may be stigmatized in ways that call into question their credibility and reliability.[41]

Attorneys should educate themselves on instances in which stigma may occur across all stages of the criminal justice system and during the legal process. Education is necessary to not only raise attorney awareness but also inform opportunities where attorneys can use their position to influence change. Attorneys can build a capacity within their organization or within their jurisdiction's criminal justice system to evoke change, if they are in the position to do so, or leverage their role to mitigate the influences of stigma in individual cases.

Attorney education should include understanding when stigmatization is likely to occur. Stigma can be seen in decision-making even if unintended. Decision-making processes that are ambiguous, rely on subjective or unstructured criteria, or allow broad discretion are easily influenced by stigma.[42] Take mental health courts, for example. They can rely on prosecutor-led referrals that provide limited structure in the eligibility determination process. This embeds subjectivity into the decision-making process. Attorney preferences for certain groups or stigma against

---

40. *Pescosolido*, *supra* note 24.

41. *Id.*

42. Judges & Psychiatrists Leadership Initiative, Idaho Judicial Conference Virtual Training: Judicial Work at the Interface of Mental Health & Criminal (Sept. 27, 2021) [hereinafter Judges & Psychiatrists Leadership Initiative].

other groups may unintentionally influence who is provided access to the court program or who is shut out of consideration.

Stigma can arise through situational triggers, such as when criminal justice professionals discriminate or are motivated by stigma under certain conditions. This can happen even if professionals would not draw upon stigma in less pressured situations. Situational triggers include situational time pressures and situational incentives. Situational time pressures occur when criminal justice professionals must make complex decisions or judgments quickly, or when professionals are distracted and cannot fully absorb and process information. When time pressures cause criminal justice professionals to rush to a decision, they are more likely to apply stigma and stereotypes to come to the decision.[43] Stereotypes and stigma are, unfortunately, an efficiency of thought. They are relied on over stereotype-inconsistent information when decisions need to be made quickly.[44] An example of this is a situation where law enforcement officers respond to a call for service involving a youth of color who has mental illness and a white youth who does not. The officers decide that arrests are needed to de-escalate the situation and officers falsely assume fault and arrest the youth of color.

Though they are different from stigma, decision-makers can express implicit biases during situational triggers that also draw out stigmatization. This includes situations where attorneys and other criminal justice professionals have limited cognitive capacity due to hunger, fatigue, multitasking, or being subject to interruption. Instances of decision-making that become habitual or intuitive, or that require a spontaneous decision, can cause attorneys and other decision-makers to rely on bias and stigma. Consider situations where decision-makers draw upon bias and stigma to inform decisions made under time pressures or when relying on their "gut feelings."[45]

---

43. Eric D. Wesselmann et al., *The Effects of Time Pressure on Controlling Reactions to Persons with Mental Illness*, 34 Basic and Applied Soc. Psych., no. 6, 2010, 565–71; Mary E. Wheeler & Susan T. Fiske, *Controlling Racial Prejudice: Social-Cognitive Goals Affect Amygdala and Stereotype Activation*, 16 Psych. Sci., no. 1, 2005, 56–63.

44. Susan T. Fiske, *Stereotyping, Prejudice, and Discrimination*, *in* 2 The Handbook of Social Psychology 357 (Daniel T. Gilbert et al. eds., 4th ed. 1998).

45. Judges & Psychiatrists Leadership Initiative, *supra* note 42.

Situational incentives occur when a quick response to a situation is encouraged over fairness and accuracy. In these situations, criminal justice professionals must process information quickly to make fast decisions. Oftentimes, they rely on automatic associations and stereotypes to inform the decision. Situational triggers cause professionals to pre-judge people or groups based on preconceived expectations that draw from stigma and often favor stereotype-confirming evidence. The stigmatized expectations can influence interactions, leading to confirmation bias. Confirmation bias is a concept that describes the tendency to investigate and process information such that it confirms preconceived attitudes, beliefs, and assumptions.[46] An example of this is an attorney who is first meeting a newly arrested and charged BIPOC adult at a bond hearing. The person may be acting unusual based on symptoms of a mental illness, of which the attorney is unaware. The attorney has worked on a lot of drug cases, which disproportionately impact BIPOC adults, and the attorney assumes the person's behavior is substance use related. The attorney confuses the context of the person's behavior with assumptions about their character. The attorney makes statements implying substance use, which triggers the person and causes them to express high emotions and catatonia. This behavior incorrectly confirms to the attorney that the person is under the influence of illicit drugs.

The Attorney's Duty of Recognition

Attorneys have many ethical and professional duties when moving criminal cases through the legal process. Complementing these duties, attorneys must recognize mental illness, stigma, and the compounding impact they have on each other. Once those harms are recognized, attorneys have a duty to mitigate them and the impact they have on cases and on the

---

46. *See, e.g.*, Barbara O'Brien, *Prime Suspect: An Examination of Factors that Aggravate and Counteract Confirmation Bias in Criminal Investigations*, 15 Psych. Pub. Pol'y & Law, no. 4, 2009, 315–44; Raymond S. Nickerson, *Confirmation Bias: A Ubiquitous Phenomenon in Many Guises*, 2 Rev. of Gen. Psych., no. 2, 1998, 175–220; Vanessa Meterko et al., *Criminal Investigations, Cognitive Bias, and Wrongful Convictions*, Innocence Project, https://www.innocenceproject.org/wp-content/uploads/2019/09/ASC-2017-poster-11.10.17_final.pdf (last visited Mar. 27, 2022).

people involved. The following chapters take the foundational concepts learned thus far and begin guiding attorneys through core competencies, skills, and practice tools that can assist with opening communication with people of diverse backgrounds who have mental illness and confronting undue influences that can impede their access to justice.

Tools and Resources

- *The Evolving Science on Implicit Bias: An Updated Resource for the State Court Community* by the National Center for State Courts.
- *The Judge's Guide to Mental Illnesses in the Courtroom* by the Judges and Psychiatrists Leadership Initiative.
- John S. Carbone, A Lawyer's Guide to Understanding Psychiatry (American Bar Association 2012).
- Mental Health First Aid courses.

PART II

How Criminal Justice Professionals Can Help Advance Equity

CHAPTER 3

Ethical Pathways to Advocacy

People of diverse backgrounds who have mental illness often have direct or indirect experiences with the criminal justice system, including experiences that extend prior to current involvement. These experiences often create mistrust of the system and potential mistrust of attorneys. Experience-based mistrust may result from power differentials inherent to the legal process and to the system itself, as well as fear of not knowing what to expect. As criminal justice professionals in most jurisdictions are predominantly white,[1] experience-based mistrust of the criminal justice system can also be triggered by overwhelmingly negative experiences with white people.

Conversely, attorneys can carry their own experiences, stigma, and biases that can cause people to distrust them and the legal process, or that can interfere with the pursuit of justice. The experiences and perspectives of attorneys can also influence interactions with other justice professionals, witnesses, and survivors of crime. Attorneys can avoid taking missteps caused by their own experiences or perspectives and can repair distrust by developing cultural competency. The tenants of cultural competency

1. *See, e.g.*, American Bar Association, *ABA Profile of the Legal Profession 2020*, 3 (2020), https://www.americanbar.org/groups/young_lawyers/projects/men-of-color/lawyer-demographics/ (last visited Mar. 27, 2022) (attorneys of color make up only 14.1 percent of all attorneys licensed to practice in the United States and its territories).

align with the ethics and professionalism standards of legal practice. In some cases, tenants of cultural competency are embedded in the framework of national and state laws and regulations that address competency in the practice of law.

This chapter examines misconceptions around race and cultural neutrality, and it clears up the misconception that cultural competency is tantamount to color blindness and that color blind practices achieve cultural competency. This is followed by an overview of cultural competency principles that can support attorneys working on cases involving people who have mental illness. Recognizing the abundance of implicit bias trainings across the field crafted specifically for attorneys, this chapter seeks to supplement, and not supplant, outside teachings on bias and racial fairness.

Race and Cultural Neutrality

Many criminal justice systems rely on color blind—or race neutral—policies, processes, programs. Race neutral practices are developed as a method to seek out racial neutrality pursuant to the belief that decision-making should not consider racial group membership or race-based differences.[2] Despite good intentions assumed in their design, race neutral practices create the illusion of racial neutrality while perpetuating racial inequities, disproportionalities, and disparities.[3] Attorneys who attempt to adopt race neutral practices make these same missteps.

Race neutral practices deny a fundamental part of people's identity and ignore the struggles that are inherent to those identities. Such practices ignore historical and structural inequities, racism, and other prejudices that impact individual experiences, and they ignore the historical

---

2. Evan P. Apfelbaum et al., *Racial Color Blindness: Emergence, Practice, and Implications*, 21 Current Directions in Psych. Sci., no. 3, 2012, 205–09.

3. *See, e.g.*, Marc Maurer, *Justice for All? Challenging Racial Disparities in the Criminal Justice System*, Am. Bar Assoc. Human Rights Magazine (Oct. 1. 2010), https://www.americanbar.org/groups/crsj/publications/human_rights_magazine_home/human_rights_vol37_2010/fall2010/justice_for_all_challenging_racial_disparities_criminal_justice_system (last visited Mar. 27, 2022).

and structural inequities inherent in the criminal justice system. This creates erasure of context. Race neutral practices fail to consider the current and sociohistorical contexts of the criminal justice and legal systems and erases or dismisses them when addressing the etiology of inequities within those systems.[4] The erasure of context is hugely consequential. While it removes the focus of race and racial inequities from decision-making, it also fails to address or correct them.

The application of race neutrality to criminal justice practices and decision-making does not cause racism, inequities, or inequalities to go away. Attorneys who seek to adopt racially neutral practices are often unaware of or refuse to acknowledge the impact of racism and inequity within the criminal justice system and the legal process. Attorneys often view the legal process through a lens shaped by unconscious and sometimes conscious bias, wealth, and privilege. This can be as obvious as an overt disconnect between words and actions, like if attorneys or decision-makers proclaim race neutrality but allow stereotypes and prejudices to sway decision-making. It can also be subtle, as shown in pursuing racially neutral disposition options that yield foreseeable and avoidable harms. Race neutral eligibility criteria that rely on subjective factors for admittance into alternatives to incarceration is a good illustration of this. The eligibility criteria may disproportionality admit certain groups of people while disproportionally shutting out other groups of people.

Just as it is important to avoid race neutral practices, it is important for attorneys to avoid culturally blind practices that seek to accomplish cultural neutrality. Culturally neutral practices ignore the language, idiomatic expressions, and other characteristics of culture. These practices may skew or influence the way attorneys perceive and define intent, credibility, criminal culpability, and reasonableness. For example, attorneys are trained to affix the plain language meaning to words and actions, but a culturally neutral application of plain language can underserve everyone involved in the case. Attorneys should recognize the

---

4. Sonya M. Shadravan & Nicolás E. Barceló, *Social Injustice and Mental Health Inequities*, *in* SOCIAL (IN)JUSTICE AND MENTAL HEALTH, 3, 4–11 (Ruth S. Shim & Sarah Y. Vinson eds., 1st ed. 2021).

relationship between plain language meaning and the contextual application of culture to actions and to words. Attorneys should assess the influence that culture has on actions and words and use that assessment to define meaning more effectively.[5]

Cultural Competency[6]

Cultural misunderstandings can impede standards of impartiality and reasonableness. To prevent this, attorneys must recognize and understand people's culture and must avoid making arbitrary and ethnocentric interpretations. These arbitrary and culturally divergent interpretations judge other people's cultures according to one's own standards. This causes attorneys to perceive other cultures as different, inferior, ignorant, or inherently immoral.[7] Cultural competency is a tool to avoid this.

Cultural competency assists attorneys in appreciating culture without placing judgment on cultural differences. Cultural competency provides attorneys with knowledge, attitudes, and skills that enable them to appreciate and work with people of diverse backgrounds. Cultural competency is important for attorneys on both sides of the courtroom. To achieve fairness under law and fairness in effectuating justice, attorneys on both sides need to appreciate the cultural uniqueness of the communities they seek to protect. Certain topics about culture or cultural impacts on mental health and criminal justice may be uncomfortable for attorneys. It is important to address these topics as they are critical to the people moving through the legal process. Cultural competency can also assist attorneys in achieving positive criminal justice and public safety outcomes.[8]

Developing cultural competency allows attorneys to examine their own biases and limited exposures to people of diverse backgrounds, and

---

5. Shiv Narayan Persaud, *Is Color Blind Justice Also Culturally Blind? The Cultural Blindness in Justice*, 14 Berkeley J. Afr. Am. L. & Pol'y 25, 2012, 23–64.

6. Unless otherwise cited, the sources for information in this section is from Substance Abuse and Mental Health Services Administration, Improving Cultural Competence A Treatment Improvement Protocol 59 (2014), https://www.ncbi.nlm.nih.gov/books/NBK207191 (last visited Mar. 27, 2022).

7. Persaud, *supra* note 5.

8. *Id.*

to address them. Cultural competency is a learned skill that takes practice. Attorneys should be committed to regularly practicing cultural competency to better advocate for equity and justice.

Cultural Competency in Social Relationships and within Systems

Cultural competency in social relationships contemplates beliefs and attitudes toward people and how those beliefs and attitudes influence personal behavior. Attorneys should recognize that everyone, including themselves, holds bias and stigma that can influence personal thoughts about or actions toward others. These biases can be overt or covert and can even exist on a subconscious level.[9] An examination of one's own biases will help identify areas that attorneys need to address to reduce negative influences on cases. Consider the ways that personal values influence expectations of people moving through the justice system and examine whether cultural misinterpretations influence these expectations. Consider what actions to take to ensure personal biases or beliefs will not influence the attorney role within the case.

An intersectional approach to cultural competency leads to an even more effective understanding of the people moving through the system. Explore the overlapping and compounding effect of people's identities on their participation in the alleged crime, their response to being a survivor of crime, and their experience moving through the criminal justice system. People of diverse backgrounds who have mental illness, for instance, may self-medicate using illicit drugs, which leads to criminal justice involvement. They hold multiple intertwined identities—Black, Indigenous, and People of Color (BIPOC), presence of mental illness, criminal justice involvement, and substance use. The general public and criminal justice professionals devalue these intertwined identities, causing people to experience increased discrimination, microaggressions, and bigotry when moving through the criminal justice system and seeking advocacy and justice through the legal process.

---

9. *See, e.g.*, American Bar Association, ABA Diversity and Inclusion 360 Commission Toolkit Introduction, https://www.americanbar.org/content/dam/aba/administrative/diversity-portal/implicitbias_toolkit.pdf (last visited Mar. 27, 2022).

The criminal justice system, as well as broader communities, often reduces the heterogeneous experiences of people of diverse backgrounds into a convenient group that is subject to stereotyping and discrimination.[10] Cultural competency interrupts this way of thinking. Cultural competency within systems and institutions contemplates the cultural inequities that exist within those entities, including historical and structural inequities and how they impact each racial group in different ways.[11] Cultural competency in this regard also contemplates the ways that inequities influence system and institution responses. The criminal justice system hosts a multitude of inequities. They range from racial disparities in who ends up being involved in the criminal justice system to racial disparities among the length of jail and prison sentences to exacerbating economic inequities through the imposition of fines and fees that disproportionately impact people of diverse backgrounds, among others.[12]

Attorneys can take action to improve cultural competency within the justice system by understanding the impact that culture and racism has on the criminal justice system itself and identifying opportunities to mitigate its impact on the people moving through it. Attorneys should consider the impact that systemic inequities and racial disparities can have on behavior, as well as the impact of historic and racialized trauma on behavior. Consider disparities that attorneys and other criminal justice professionals risk perpetuating.[13]

Court Culture, Criminal Cases, and Cultural Competency

A common misconception that attorneys should recognize is the long-held belief that the legal system and the court are free of social influences.

---

10. Hillary Potter, Intersectionality and Criminology: Disrupting and Revolutionizing Studies of Crime 3, 32 (Routledge, 1st ed., 2015).

11. *See* Mary Butler et al., *Improving Cultural Competence to Reduce Health Disparities*, Comparative Effectiveness Rev., no. 170, 2016.

12. *See* Substance Abuse and Mental Health Services Administration, The Impact of Structural Racism on Mental Health, https://mhttcnetwork.org/sites/default/files/2021-04/MHTTC_StructuralRacism_Final.pdf (last visited (Mar. 27, 2022). *See generally Racial Disparities and Dynamics in the Criminal Justice System*, National Institute of Corrections (Feb. 9, 2022), https://nicic.gov/racial-disparities-and-dynamics-criminal-justice-system.

13. Potter, *supra* note 10.

There is the presumption in the legal profession that court users hold culture while the court itself is devoid of culture. This presumption obscures realities experienced by court personnel and court users and is contrary to modern efforts to improve access to the courts and fairness in legal process.

Court systems have cultures that were and continue to be shaped by a multitude of factors—from historical and formal structures to administrative practices and policies, and even informal practices and customs. Like other public systems and institutions, the court system is not immune from influences rooted in historical and structural inequities. Exclusions that historically prohibited people of diverse backgrounds from engaging in the legal process,[14] for example, set social standards that continue to resonate today about who is traditionally represented in positions of power and vested with decision-making authority—such as attorneys and judges—and who is traditionally characterized as offenders or defendants. Even with the evolutions and innovations over time to improve access to and fairness in the courts, court culture often upholds practices, assumptions, and traditions that institutionalize whiteness as a default.

The behaviors and operations that inform the ways courts operate and how cases are resolved often rely on a "conventional court" default that is based on traditional federal and state court decorum. The default assumes normalness and otherness. This assumes that the court is normal and carries default customs and etiquettes. It assumes that anyone

---

14. For example, the U.S. legal system has a storied history of race-based jury exclusion and racial bias in jury selection (*see, e.g.*, Strauder v. West Virginia, 100 U.S. 303 (1880); Batson v. Kentucky, 476 U.S. 79 (1986); and Flowers v. Mississippi, 588 U.S. __ (2019), where the Supreme Court addressed racial discrimination in criminal proceedings and struck down racial discrimination in jury selection); race-based testimony exclusion laws (*see, e.g.*, STATUTES OF CALIFORNIA, THE CRIMINAL ACT OF 1850, STATS. 1850, ch. 99, § 14, p. 230; People v. Howard, 17 Cal. 63 (1860); and People v. Hall, 4 Cal. 399 (1854), which excluded BIPOC from testifying in court, with a state bill later legalizing testimony by Black people in 1863 (Shirley Ann Wilson Moore, *We Feel the Want of Protection: The Politics of Law and Race in California, 1848–1878*, *in* TAMING THE ELEPHANT: POLITICS, GOVERNMENT, AND LAW IN PIONEER CALIFORNIA, 118 (John F. Burns & Richard J. Orsi eds., 1st ed. 2003) and all other Indigenous and people of color receiving the right to provide testimony upon the ratification of the Fourteenth Amendment in 1868 (U.S. CONST. AMEND. XIV, § 1.)).

moving through the legal process who does not carry the court-prescribed customs and etiquettes is an outsider or faulty or otherwise does not belong. This sense of otherness dictates the perception of courts and legal processes that are outside of the norm. While conventional courts establish the default, they presume inadequacy in and question the legitimacy of other legal processes for achieving justice. Consider tribal courts. They are courts of law that many in the legal profession see as being different. Tribal courts, just like conventional courts, serve the purpose and goal of providing justice. They highlight that courts of all types have a culture. Attorneys, and other court personnel, should realize the emphasized need to acknowledge court culture when moving cases through the legal process and infuse cultural responses.[15]

Conventional court culture creates power dynamics that can require careful navigation in seeking cultural competency. Reflect on the ways that power dynamics and privilege can affect the interpretation of behavior and interpretations made by decision-makers during the legal process. Examine whether cultural misperceptions or misinterpretations of individual characteristics lead to unwarranted perceptions of increased risk and dangerousness. Consider if the presence of mental illness compounds with cultural misunderstandings to affect opinions about risk and dangerousness. Recognize that needs, including criminogenic needs, are different from risks. Needs inform the services and interventions that can help people achieve success, and risks inform the likelihood of re-offending or likelihood to not appear in court.

Attorneys who incorporate interventions designed to address risks and needs as part of disposition options should reconceptualize their understanding of each intervention and examine its effectiveness across populations. Appreciate that interventions may not be validated to prove effective with people who have mental illness and that interventions may fall short of responding to the needs of people of diverse backgrounds or

---

15. *See, e.g.*, Center for Court Innovation, Cultural Responsiveness & the Courts, https://www.courtinnovation.org/sites/default/files/documents/Cultural_Responsiveness_0.pdf#:~:text=Perhaps%20most%20significant%20in%20creating%20courts%20that%20are,biases%20and%20engaging%20with%20individuals%20from%20all%20backgrounds (last visited Mar. 27, 2022).

fail in being culturally responsive.[16] Evidence-based practices, for example, are frequently used within legal processes and case dispositions to redirect criminal thinking. Many interventions, however, are not evaluated for efficacy among people of diverse backgrounds or among people who have mental illness, and the interventions may cause people to experience negative outcomes.[17] There are many interventions that are appropriate and successful for people of diverse backgrounds. Attorneys should ensure interventions used are appropriate and are culturally responsive.

Reconceptualize approaches to interpreting the causes of crime, culpability, and criminal thinking. The criminal justice system often interprets the causes of crime and criminal thinking through a lens informed by a default white experience. Attorneys should examine whether false beliefs, such as biological determinism and cultural determinism, may influence unwarranted interpretations. Biological determinism is the false belief that racial groups are biologically and genetically different. Cultural determinism is the false belief that racial inequities are the result of people's culture.[18] Consider that the beliefs and attitudes that may drive people from diverse backgrounds to engage in unlawful behavior may be rooted in experiences of marginalization and discrimination. These experiences are outside of the default experience. Because of this, the criminal justice system often deems them as faulty or irrational rather than acknowledging that they are a product of historical and structural inequities and traumas.

Putting Cultural Competency into Practice

There are culturally competent approaches that attorneys can quickly put into practice. Coming from a place of sincere curiosity rather than judgment, attorneys can invite people to share their experiences to learn

---

16. For instance, the validation studies for evidence-based programs and interventions may not control for race, mental illness, gender, or other personal characteristics that can impact responsiveness. This infuses ambiguity into the program effectiveness across people carrying those characteristics.

17. Potter, *supra* note 10, 3, 32.

18. Ruth S. Shimm & Sarah Y. Vinson, *Social (In)Justice and Mental Health*, *in* Social (In) Justice and Mental Health, 3, 4–11 (Ruth S. Shim & Sarah Y. Vinson eds., 1st ed. 2021).

what influences may have informed their behavior. Focus on individual perspectives rather than interpreting the validity or rationality of what is being said based on one's own experiences, beliefs, or values. Seek to understand individual points of view. Be receptive to viewpoints on race, identity, and intersectionality, and be receptive of their influence on individual beliefs. Even if attorneys cannot directly understand the experiences for themselves, or may have never been witness to these experiences, attorneys should validate the feelings and experiences of others. Attorneys should acknowledge that society does not always treat people fairly. Rather than challenging people's beliefs, leverage the attorney role to challenge inequity in the criminal justice system and to pursue culturally responsive disposition options.

Attorneys can work with people to understand what they think and believe about the legal system, and what they think about the public or private mental health systems with which they may become involved. Their cultural and intersectional identities, their family, and their social environments may influence their beliefs. This may include being from a traditionally marginalized and resource-poor community. Invite people to talk about the common experiences and beliefs that others have about people like them, and how that may shape their beliefs about themselves or shape their behaviors. Ask them how they expect to be treated within the criminal justice and mental health systems, including expectations based on their cultural background and their experiences with mental illness. Invite them to share the types of resources they typically have access to that may benefit the outcome of the case and what barriers—including structural and systemic barriers—they anticipate facing.

Attorneys should self-reflect on their own personal approaches and lawyering style. Challenge circumstances where it may be uncomfortable for attorneys to ask about or discuss race, particularly if attorneys are comfortable being in homogenous environments or comfortable with achieving homogenous outcomes.[19] Understand what values attorneys bring to the case and what values their office may carry. Examine what

19. Potter, *supra* note 10.

values or beliefs people moving through the legal system may have about attorneys, the attorney role, and the attorneys' office.

Regardless of the role in the case, attorneys should identify what actions they can take to ensure cultural responsiveness, cultural competency, and equitable outcomes. Identify the types of resources and legal options that are available, including referrals to alternatives to incarceration, diversion, community or in-custody mental health treatment, or other resources that meet mental health needs. Examine those resources to ensure they are culturally responsive and will reduce rather than reproduce inequities and harm. Identify what attributes attorneys encompass that can bring about change, including change in the case at hand, change across greater proportions of cases, and change across the greater criminal justice system.

Throughout the practice of cultural competency, it can be helpful to undertake self-assessment on a routine basis. Self-assessment can assist attorneys in recognizing advancement within personal cultural competency goals and to identify areas for improvements. Self-assessment questions can include the following:

- Have I recognized a bias that I have about certain people?
- Have I considered how the criminal justice and legal systems impact people of diverse backgrounds and diverse communities?
- Have I considered how the mental health system impacts people of diverse backgrounds and diverse communities?
- Have I attended a cultural competency or elimination of bias training?
- Have I sought education or guidance about a racial or cultural issue that arose in a case?
- Have I reflected on how racial and cultural identity affected a case?
- How do I see cultural backgrounds influencing communication, including influences in how I communicate with people and in how they communicate with me?
- Have I considered the ways in which decisions about a case have affected people of diverse backgrounds or communities?

- Have I challenged a biased statement or impact (my own or that of someone else)?
- Have I challenged race or culturally neutral/color-blind practices?
- Do I recognize when a case or potential disposition option may ignore or perpetuate existing inequities or produce unintended consequences?
- Do I make an express effort to advance equity in my cases?

Words Matter

Complementing cultural competency is linguistic competency and the specific focus of word choices. Words are a foundational tool in lawyering. Words have the ability to change how people think about and view situations. Words that attorneys use have a profound impact on the pursuit of equity, fairness, and the perception of justice. This extends to words used in the courtroom, when talking with opposing counsel or other criminal justice professionals, and when talking to people involved in the criminal justice system—including people charged with crimes, survivors of crime, and witnesses.

Words can create or destroy trust, encourage or deter collaboration and engagement, and advocate for justice or impose prejudice. While there are techniques common to specific attorney roles, such as prosecution or defense, using respectful and mindful word choices will not diminish the role of the attorney or alter criminal proceedings. Mindful word choices will not impede advisory or adversary roles and will not diminish the adversarial system. Comment 1 to Rule 1.3 of the American Bar Association's *Model Rules of Professional Conduct* articulates this concept well. It states that the duty of an attorney "does not require the use of offensive tactics or preclude the treating of all persons involved in the legal process with courtesy and respect."[20]

The words that attorneys use take on meaningful roles. They can be neutral or charged, and they can bring up positive or negative associations

20. American Bar Association, Rule 1.3 Diligence – Comment, Model Rules of Professional Conduct, https://www.americanbar.org/groups/professional_responsibility/publications/model_rules_of_professional_conduct/rule_1_3_diligence/comment_on_rule_1_3/ (last visited Mar. 27, 2022).

in the speaker or in the people who hear or read them. In reference to people involved in the criminal justice and mental health systems, words draw correlation to people, places, or institutions. The correlations can help identify someone or someplace through positive or neutral interpretation. This correlation can also devalue or assign negative connotations.[21] Attorneys must be intentional with their words to avoid unduly prejudicing decision-making and impeding the fair administration of justice.

Linguistic and cultural competency are vital to avoiding stereotyping, discrimination, and stigmatization. Linguistic competency centers on the ability to understand, appreciate, and effectively interact with people whose language, culture, or belief systems are different from one's own. Alongside cultural competency, this includes using correct terms to refer to racial identity and intersectional identities. It also recognizes that there may be occasions where it is appropriate to identify racial, intersectional, or cultural identities. There may also be occasions where it would be inappropriate to do so. Acknowledge that using socially accepted labels to identify people or groups often causes harm and can create a barrier to effective interaction. It is best for attorneys to understand the people and the communities involved in or impacted by their work and by their jurisdiction's criminal justice system. Linguistic competency recognizes that terminology preferences can vary by person or by community. If there is uncertainty, it is helpful for attorneys to ask people directly about their preferred terms and language customs or to ask others who are knowledgeable.[22]

Word choice is also important when drawing up associations or identifying people beyond the cultural context. Words should presume innocence. Words should be respectful and should avoid labeling or stigmatization. Remember that language attached to stigma or negative connotations is amplified when affixed to people of diverse backgrounds. Attorneys should ensure that no discriminating or stigmatizing language

---

21. Kyle Hildebrant & Ryan Durant, *Why We Name: The Power of Taming to Drive Deep Connections with a Brand*, OVO, https://brandsbyovo.com/why-we-name-drive-connections-with-brand/ (last visited Mar. 27, 2022).

22. *Communicating With and About People with Disabilities*, CDC, https://www.cdc.gov/ncbddd/disabilityandhealth/materials/factsheets/fs-communicating-with-people.html (last visited Mar. 27, 2022).

is used to pursue a conviction. This includes avoiding the use of charged language and intentionally misattributing race, gender, and other social labels as a litigation technique, and avoiding language that may encourage conviction by teasing out the sensationalized fear or bias of jurors or other factfinders.

Minding word choice includes moving away from outdated and problematic terminology. Attorneys should use words that recognize mental illness and trauma and that accurately and respectfully refer to them. This includes the use of "people first language," which emphasizes the person first rather than their disability, medical condition, or situation.[23] Use the term "people who have mental illness" instead of "mentally ill people." Words should convey impartiality rather than reducing people to their criminal status. Use the term "people convicted of crimes" instead of "convicts" or "felons." Use "people involved in the criminal justice system" instead of "inmates" or "offenders." When addressing people directly, use their preferred name and pronouns. Use "John Doe" instead of referring to them as "defendant" or other criminal justice labels. Use their chosen name instead of deadnaming. Deadnaming is the harmful act of referring to people who are transgender or nonbinary by a name that they used prior to their transition. There may be other occasions where people have a chosen name that is different from their name at birth and when it would be harmful for attorneys to use the incorrect name. Name change during the naturalization process, for instance, may enable people immigrating to the United States to select a name that is reflective of their identity.

Moving Forward with Cultural Competency

While the criminal justice system often strives to achieve neutrality in its processes and responses, ignoring race and culture arbitrarily disregards the lived experiences of the people moving through it. This creates disparate criminal justice impacts and lessens the impartiality and effectiveness of the legal process. Attorneys can combat these adverse impacts by

23. *Id.*; *State Court Behavioral Health Series*, NATIONAL CENTER FOR STATE COURTS, https://courses.ncsc.org/course/behavioralhealth (last visited Mar. 27, 2022).

practicing cultural competency and by mastering the art of words and language. Cultural competency is important to the role of the attorney and in upholding due process and the rule of law. Cultural competency takes time and evolves as attorneys learn and improve through practice. Cultural competency when working on cases involving people of diverse backgrounds who have mental illness recognizes that their individual values, attitudes, and beliefs shape their involvement in crime and their responses to being a witness or survivor of crime. It is the duty of attorneys to respect their values, attitudes, and beliefs and to act ethically and equitably in pursuing justice.

Tools and Resources

- *Communicating With and About People with Disabilities* by the Centers for Disease Control and Prevention.
- The National Association of Counties, *Diversity, Equity and Inclusion Key Terms and Definition.*
- *The Enhancing Equity in the Criminal Justice System: A Self-Reflection Tool* by SAMHSA's GAINS Center for Behavioral Health and Justice Transformation.
- *Improving Cultural Competency: Working with People in the Criminal Justice System Who Have Mental Illnesses* webinar recording by the Judges' and Psychiatrists' Leadership Initiative in collaboration with the American Bar Association.
- *Wrestling with Words, Acronyms & Language in Antiracism Advocacy and Actions* webinar by the American Bar Association Section of Civil Rights and Social Justice.

CHAPTER 4

Establishing Lawyering Tools for Advancing Equity

It is the duty of attorneys to do no harm. However, attorneys and people involved in criminal cases can view the legal process and what it means to achieve justice differently. Attorneys often interpret justice through different life experiences, privileges, and levels of understanding of historical inequities, theory, and other contexts than the people involved in criminal cases. It is the responsibility of attorneys to realize these differences and to consider the impact that their decisions, and the law, will have on everyone affected.

Attorneys must exercise professional judgment that recognizes the power of attorneys and the power of the law. They must act with the intention and humility to listen and learn from people involved in cases and to act accordingly. Approaches such as trauma-informed lawyering and motivational interviewing embrace this notion. Understanding the basics of trauma can assist attorneys in building trust, fostering receptiveness, and mastering communication. These strategies can help improve justice and legal outcomes while reducing conflict and challenges that may otherwise take place during the legal process. Commonly adopted by attorneys and incorporated into court systems and administrative policies, these approaches provide effective skills that attorneys can easily incorporate into everyday practice.

The Trauma-Informed Lawyer

People involved in the juvenile and adult criminal justice systems have high rates of mental illness and personal histories of trauma.[1] Of people moving through the criminal justice system, people of diverse backgrounds who have mental illness experience trauma at such high rates that trauma is considered a universal experience for them.[2] This pervasiveness and the impacts that trauma has on each case require attorneys to recognize and respond to trauma. Attorneys can do this through practicing trauma-informed lawyering.

Trauma-informed lawyering is a multifaceted approach that can improve attorney interactions with people of diverse backgrounds who have mental illness. Attorneys can use trauma-informed lawyering when interacting with people charged with crimes, witnesses, and survivors of crime. It recognizes the role that trauma plays in people's lives,[3] the role of trauma in interactions with attorneys, and the role that attorneys can take to reduce re-traumatization. Trauma-informed lawyering equips attorneys with tools that can lead to more effective interactions, and can lead to improved public safety, improved health outcomes, and reduced recidivism.[4]

Trauma-informed lawyering should be the expectation, not the exception. Trauma-informed lawyering serves the entire courtroom and upholds the adversarial nature of the legal process. Trauma-informed lawyering enhances the attorney role. It does not diminish the role of prosecutors or defense attorneys, nor does it encourage them to adopt a social

---

1. Substance Abuse and Mental Health Services Administration's Trauma and Justice Strategic Initiative, SAMHSA's Concept of Trauma and Guidance for a Trauma-Informed Approach (2014) [hereinafter Trauma and Guidance for a Trauma-Informed Approach].

2. Substance Abuse and Mental Health Services Administration, Essential Components of Trauma-Informed Judicial Practice (2013) [hereinafter Essential Components].

3. Maxine Harris & Roger D. Fallot, *Envisioning a Trauma-Informed Service System: A Vital Paradigm Shift, in Trauma-Informed Systems, in* 89 Using Trauma Theory to Design Service Symptoms 83, 84 (Maxine Harris & Roger D. Fallot eds., 2001).

4. *Trauma Training for Criminal Justice Professionals*, Substance Abuse and Mental Health Services Administration's GAINS Center, https://www.samhsa.gov/gains-center/trauma-training-criminal-justice-professionals (last visited Mar. 27, 2022).

work approach to their role. Instead, trauma-informed lawyering allows prosecutors to meet ethical standards, and to fairly exercise prosecutorial functions.[5] It assists prosecutors with conducting thorough investigations, making informed credibility determinations, and making informed discretionary decisions.[6] For defense attorneys, trauma-informed lawyering avoids re-traumatization that the attorney-client relationship may otherwise cause. It provides defense attorneys with opportunities to improve connections with clients, and to improve advocacy.

What Is Trauma?

The American Psychological Association defines trauma as "an emotional response to a terrible event." Survivors of trauma can experience long-term trauma responses. They can experience behavioral symptoms such as heightened emotions and flashbacks of the traumatic events, and physical symptoms such as neurological issues and substance use.[7] There are different types of traumas, and trauma can affect an individual, a group, a community, or an entire culture.

Trauma can be experienced through a single event or across multiple events, or it can endure over a long period of time. Trauma can be a result of a natural event, such as a natural disaster, or result from a human-created event, such as war, structural inequities, or physical injury resulting from self-induced harm or from victimization.[8] The types of traumas experienced by people involved in the criminal justice system are numerous and may be compounded. They include being victims/survivors of a crime, physical injury, experiencing structural or individual racism or

---

5. Trauma Informed Prosecution Presentation, Institute for Innovation in Prosecution at John Jay College of Criminal Justice, https://www.prosecution.org/s/IIP-Trauma-Informed-Prosecution.pptx (last visited Mar. 27, 2022) [hereinafter Trauma Informed Prosecution Presentation].

6. *Id.*

7. *Trauma*, American Psychological Association, https://www.apa.org/topics/trauma (last visited Mar. 27, 2022); Substance Abuse and Mental Health Services Administration, Trauma-Informed Care in Behavioral Health Services Treatment Improvement Protocol 57 (2014), https://www.ncbi.nlm.nih.gov/books/NBK207191 (last visited Mar. 27, 2022) [hereinafter Treatment Improvement Protocol 57].

8. Treatment Improvement Protocol 57, *supra* note 7.

stigmatization, or experiencing adverse childhood experiences.[9] Adverse childhood experiences can be the direct cause of future victimization or future criminal engagement.[10] System-oriented trauma can stem from incarceration or involuntary hospitalization. Moving through the legal process, and the stress of the courtroom, can re-traumatize and impair survivors' ability to communicate effectively with attorneys, judges, and other criminal justice professionals.[11]

Trauma is experienced directly or indirectly. A common example of this is being a victim of sexual assault, witnessing extrajudicial police killing, or unwarranted use of force. Survivors of trauma experience traumatic stress. Symptoms of traumatic stress include cognitive and other psychological responses. Traumatic stress may be ever-present or triggered by certain events. Cultural interpretations and cultural responses to trauma can influence trauma responses and how they are managed. The way survivors deal with traumatic stress and the extent to which survivors internalize or communicate trauma to others may vary based on cultural norms or cultural responses.[12]

Although anyone can experience trauma, there are individual and sociocultural factors that increase the risk of experiencing trauma. Social, demographic, environmental, and psychological factors influence risk. These factors also influence the extent of trauma responses. They can influence the severity of traumatic stress reactions and long-term physical, emotional, and cultural consequences. Severe traumatic stress responses are common among people who have a history of prior psychological trauma, people who have mental illness, people experiencing homelessness, people of diverse backgrounds, and people who identify as women, transgender, nonbinary, genderqueer, lesbian, gay, or bisexual.[13]

---

9. Essential Components, *supra* note 2.
10. *Adverse Childhood Experiences (ACEs)*, Center for Disease Control and Prevention, https://www.cdc.gov/violenceprevention/aces/index.html (last visited Mar. 27, 2022). *See, e.g.*, Justice Analytical Services, The Scottish Government, What have ACEs got to do with Justice?, Understanding Childhood Adversity, Resilience and Crime (2018).
11. Essential Components, *supra* note 2.
12. Treatment Improvement Protocol 57, *supra* note 7.
13. *Id.*

Importantly, trauma can significantly impact survivors, regardless of whether survivors are diagnosed with a traumatic stress disorder or would meet the criteria for a diagnosis.[14]

Trauma and Culture

Culture can impact the way people deal with trauma, both throughout the duration of the traumatic event and after it passes.[15] Cultural awareness allows attorneys to appreciate that survivors of trauma who are impacted by the criminal justice system have experiences that are informed by their cultural background and cultural identities. The cultural backgrounds of attorneys and other criminal justice professionals also impact survivors. Cultural backgrounds include racial and ethnic identity, self or familial immigration status, and nationality, among other identities. Like cultural competency, developing cultural awareness can take time.

Attorneys can begin developing cultural awareness by seeing people as individuals in addition to recognizing their cultural backgrounds. People of diverse backgrounds, including those who have mental illness, are not monoliths. Their experiences may be different from others who share their identities. Recognize people's cultural background and other background characteristics that may apply to them and avoid reducing them to those impersonal labels.[16] Recognize that people's cultural background may impact the way they are treated by criminal justice and mental health professionals, including attorneys, judges, and jurors.[17] People's background can influence the way they perceive their involvement in and progression through those systems. People may be afraid, untrusting, or ambivalent about the criminal justice system and the legal process,

---

14. *State Court Behavioral Health Series*, National Center for State Courts, https://courses.ncsc.org/course/behavioralhealth (last visited Mar. 27, 2022) [hereinafter *State Court Behavioral Health Series*].

15. Treatment Improvement Protocol 57, *supra* note 7.

16. *State Court Behavioral Health Series*, *supra* note 14.

17. Office of the Surgeon General et al, Mental Health: Culture, Race, and Ethnicity: A Supplement to Mental Health: A Report of the Surgeon General (2001), https://www.ncbi.nlm.nih.gov/books/NBK44249/ (last visited Mar. 27, 2022).

and the legal process may also be a traumatizing or retraumatizing event for them.[18]

Developing cultural awareness requires appreciation that diverse communities and other traditionally marginalized communities experience trauma that is rooted in historical and structural inequities. These inequities cause people to have reduced social opportunities. Inequities include lack of access to quality education, housing, and health care. These communities are also over-policed and overrepresented in the criminal justice system, including over-incarcerated. [19] They also experience structural violence, which puts them in situations and conditions that increases their likelihood of experiencing or witnessing violence.[20] Encounters with the criminal justice system include direct and vicarious interactions. The criminal justice system itself has historically created and exacerbated trauma of diverse communities. When people from diverse backgrounds become involved in the criminal justice system, they carry this trauma with them, and that trauma can impair their ability or willingness to trust and work with attorneys.[21]

A Starting Point for Trauma-Informed Lawyering

There is not a sequential process for practicing trauma-informed lawyering but, as with any relationship, trauma-informed lawyering requires building trust and rapport. When first meeting people, attorneys should begin by introducing themselves and describing their role in the case. Identify other people who may come into the case or engage with them. Identify other attorneys, investigators, mental health evaluators, or other experts used in the case. Address people by their given or preferred names, and avoid destigmatizing language, such as by using people-first

---

18. Trauma Informed Prosecution Presentation, *supra* note 5; Trauma and Guidance for a Trauma-Informed Approach, *supra* note 1; *State Court Behavioral Health Series*, *supra* note 14.

19. Trauma Informed Prosecution Presentation, *supra* note 5; Trauma and Guidance for a Trauma-Informed Approach, *supra* note 1; *State Court Behavioral Health Series*, *supra* note 14.

20. American Medical Association, Organizational Strategic Plan to Embed Racial Justice and Advance Health Equity 2021–2023, 21(2021).

21. *State Court Behavioral Health Series*, *supra* note 14.

language.[22] Personalize the interaction so people know they are seen as individuals rather than as their condition or their criminal justice status.

When talking to people, regardless of their traumatic stress reaction or mental ability, treat them age appropriately. If people are at the age of adulthood, treat them as an adult. Avoid talking down to them.[23] Depending on the nature of the first meeting, it may be helpful to begin with questions or conversations that will not trigger emotional or anxious responses. Explain the nature and nuance of the legal process, and explain the nature and reason for questions. Be strategic about what information will help the case and what information may be helpful down the road.[24] Use open-ended questions and avoid leading questions. Consider the impact of the meeting environment and atmosphere, including the physical space.[25] Consider comfort or stress levels if meeting in jail or in office settings. Consider the social atmosphere, such as comfort with attorneys and other professionals who participate in the case.[26] Be respectfully curious about people's lived experience, and ask questions from a place of compassionate interest instead of from a place of judgment.[27] As trust builds, encourage people to be more honest and forthcoming in providing needed information.

Trauma-Informed Communication

Attorneys are effective communicators, and trauma-informed lawyering encourages practices that can enhance engagement. Attorneys should monitor the speed and tone of their speech and be tactful when asking questions.[28] Enunciate, speak slowly and clearly, and provide ample

22. *Id.*

23. The ARC et al., Victims, Witnesses, and Defendants with Mental Illness or Intellectual and Developmental Disabilities: A Guide for Prosecutors (2020).

24. *State Court Behavioral Health Series*, *supra* note 14.

25. *Id.*; Treatment Improvement Protocol 57, *supra* note 7; Trauma Informed Prosecution Presentation, *supra* note 5; Trauma and Guidance for a Trauma-Informed Approach, *supra* note 1.

26. *See, e.g.*, Trauma and Guidance for a Trauma-Informed Approach, *supra* note 1.

27. Trauma Informed Prosecution Presentation, *supra* note 5; *State Court Behavioral Health Series*, *supra* note 14.

28. *State Court Behavioral Health Series*, *supra* note 14.

time for people to respond. Provide information that is easy to follow. Be aware of any difficulties that people may have in understanding legal concepts or strategies. Consider paraphrasing complex legal concepts. Translate legal concepts from legalese to layperson terms, including using familiar language.[29] Attorneys should practice active listening. Active listening allows attorneys to listen with the intent to fully appreciate what is said, rather than listening with the intent to reply.[30] This includes asking open-ended questions, mirroring people's words and body language, and reflecting back to them the information they provided.[31]

A mindful approach to body language is important. Display a patient and empathizing demeanor. Consider opportunities to reduce power dynamics. Power dynamics can be reminiscent of abuse dynamics that survivors experienced during traumatic events, and power dynamics can hinder engagement.[32] Reducing power dynamics can involve removing suit jackets, opening body language by uncrossing arms and orientating the body toward people, sitting at the same level as them, and looking them in the eye.[33] Be conscious of people's behaviors and etiquettes. It is also important to understand cultural responses that may be important or apply to them.[34] Attorneys may want to conduct advance research, if appropriate. There may be cultural norms, for instance, that dictate whether people maintain eye contact or "talk with their hands."

Avoiding Miscommunication

An important aspect of trauma-informed lawyering is identifying roadblocks or setbacks during interactions should they arise. If roadblocks arise, take measures to get the conversation back on track. This takes practice. Recognize people's intersectional identities and the stigma and

---

29. *Id.*

30. Active listening is a key skill utilized in the motivational interviewing approach described later in this chapter.

31. *State Court Behavioral Health Series*, *supra* note 14.

32. Harris & Fallot, *supra* note 3.

33. Trauma Informed Prosecution Presentation, *supra* note 5; *State Court Behavioral Health Series*, *supra* note 14

34. Treatment Improvement Protocol 57, *supra* note 7.

discrimination they may face. People may be hesitant to answer questions that directly ask if they have experienced trauma or traumatic events.[35] Ask strategic questions to help people identify and open up about their trauma and trauma responses.[36] For instance, witnesses or survivors of crime may hesitate when asked direct questions about the circumstances leading to their involvement in the case. They may better respond to questions that slowly approach their involvement. Ask questions such as "Have you seen someone getting arrested?" or "Have you seen someone get physically attacked?"

Attorneys should be mindful of structural barriers and sociocultural influences that may be factors in traumatic events or trauma responses.[37] Barriers and influences may have affected past or current attempts to access treatment for mental illness or for traumatic stress responses. Recognize the ways that these experiences may affect people. People may fail to recognize the impact that trauma has had on them. People may have experience-based fear and experience-based mistrust of health and social support systems or of the criminal justice system. These experiences may also cause people to fear being vulnerable in the community or when incarcerated.[38] People may fear being vulnerable with attorneys.

Attorneys should recognize scenarios that may impede communication and take steps to minimize them. If trauma caused a failure of recognition or other cognition difficulties leading to misunderstanding, attorneys can address the issue by asking open-ended questions to help people recall requested information.[39] To overcome experience-based mistrust of attorneys or of the criminal justice system, attorneys should build further rapport through a relational approach.[40] If people express guilt

---

35. *State Court Behavioral Health Series*, *supra* note 14.
36. Lisa Callahan et al., *Fostering Trauma-Informed Practices in Your Courtroom: Approaches for Judges, Court Staff, and Providers*, Substance and Mental Health Services Administration webinar (May 26, 2021).
37. Treatment Improvement Protocol 57, *supra* note 7.
38. Niki A. Miller & Lisa M. Najavits, *Creating Trauma-informed Correctional Care: A Balance of Goals and Environment*, 3 European J. Pychotraumatology (2012).
39. *State Court Behavioral Health Series*, *supra* note 14; Treatment Improvement Protocol 57, *supra* note 7.
40. Jill Howieson & Shane L. Rogers, *Rethinking the Lawyer-Client Interview: Taking a Relational Approach*, 26 Psychiatry Psych. & L. 659–68 (2019).

or shame of their trauma or mental illness, or express denial, attorneys should be empathetic and nonjudgmental. When appropriate, recall collateral information, such as mental health records, to help jog their thinking.[41] In any situation involving miscommunication, remain calm and do not take people's frustrations personally.

De-Escalation

Effective trauma-informed lawyering involves being prepared to de-escalate tense situations and heightened emotions should they arise. Decisions made during these situations can be negatively perceived and can create distrust of attorneys or the legal system. Try to identify triggers of escalated emotions if they are not immediately obvious. Employ verbal and nonverbal de-escalation techniques.[42]

Verbal de-escalation techniques include intentional listening to better understand what people are trying to communicate and to understand the cause of the heightened emotions. Move toward intentional listening by calming their communication style. Attorneys can lower their voice, slow down, and ask simple, open-ended questions. Give people ample time to respond to questions without interruption. Once people are finished speaking, let them know if further clarification is needed. Reflect back what is said to show that they are heard. Nonverbal de-escalation techniques include maintaining appropriate eye contact and taking advantage of whatever space may be available in the physical environment.[43] For instance, allow people more personal space if possible.

De-escalation is a helpful technique for people experiencing symptoms of mental illness or trauma who could benefit from grounding. Practice patience and empathy. Refrain from getting frustrated by the situation, and do not take irritating or offensive behavior personally or view them as manipulative. Understand that people's actions—behaviors, reactions, comments, and mannerisms—may result from their mental

41. *State Court Behavioral Health Series*, *supra* note 14.
42. *Id.*
43. *Id.*

illness or trauma. Do not minimize their symptoms or be dismissive. Do not argue the validity of symptoms, such as delusions or hallucinations. Instead, validate their perspective and provide support. Afterall, delusions and hallucinations are real to them and a part of their experience in the present moment. Do not argue with statements that may be unusual. If helpful, ask them to provide more detail about the statements. Avoid confrontation or making threats of any nature, such as threatening to pursue unfavorable disposition options out of frustration of the situation. Work in collaboration with them to seek a solution or resolution to the situation. Deflect if necessary, and work with them to ensure that they understand the process and do not feel hopeless in their situation.[44]

Advising Clients

Trauma-informed lawyering for defense attorneys or reentry counsel includes techniques focused on advising clients and ensuring a collaborative process. When providing legal advice, ensure that people understand the information and offer clarification if needed. Ask for their opinion and perspective, and listen reflectively by mirroring what was said. Allow them a sense of autonomy. Ensure that they feel involved in the process and empowered to help strategize their choices.[45] This can help lead to positive perceptions of the legal process regardless of case outcome.

Attorneys should also become familiar with local mental health terms and community mental health centers. This knowledge may assist attorneys in building trust by showing that attorneys are familiar with working with people who have mental illness, and that the person is not alone. This knowledge base should include familiarity with the names of local mental health clinics, psychiatric units in local jails and prisons, mental health urgent cares, emergency response units, and police and mental health co-responder programs. Familiarity should also include the names of community-based providers, peer support groups, respite centers, and other support centers.

44. *Id.*
45. *Id.*

Motivational Interviewing Basics

Motivational interviewing assists attorneys in adopting a trauma-informed practice, particularly if an interpersonal communication style is needed to break through setbacks in communication and prevent power imbalances.[46] Motivational interviewing is a collaborative, person-centered conversation style that seeks to guide intrinsic motivation to change by exploring and resolving ambivalence.[47] Motivational interviewing looks at self-perception and appreciates that people are less or more willing to change behaviors based on how they talk about them. Focusing on the positive, motivational interviewing guides people through thinking about the benefits of changing their behavior and steers them toward voicing the argument for change.[48] Although motivational interviewing was first used in clinical and social work settings, there is legitimacy for use of the approach by attorneys on both sides of the courtroom. Motivational interviewing does not change the dynamic between attorneys and people moving through the criminal justice system, nor does it change the adversarial nature of the legal process. The approach, instead, provides another tool for attorneys to improve communication when working with people of diverse backgrounds who have mental illness.

Motivational interviewing was developed in the 1980s as an intervention for people who have substance use disorders.[49] It focused on people who were resistant to reducing and abstaining from substance use, and who were resistant to addressing behaviors leading to substance use. The conversation style has since been adopted and applied to other populations that may be resistant to change, including people involved in the criminal justice system, people who have mental illness, and people

46. *Id.*
47. Substance Abuse and Mental Health Services Administration, Enhancing Motivation for Change in Substance Use Disorder Treatment: UPDATED 2019 Treatment Improvement Protocol 35 (2019), https://www.ncbi.nlm.nih.gov/books/NBK571068/ (last visited Mar. 27, 2022) [hereinafter Treatment Improvement Protocol 35].
48. *Id.*
49. Projects for Assistance in Transition from Homelessness et al., Spotlight on PATH Practices and Programs Motivational Interviewing 3 (2010), https://www.samhsa.gov/sites/default/files/programs_campaigns/homelessness_programs_resources/path-spotlight-motivational-interviewing.pdf (last visited Mar. 27, 2022).

accessing various legal and social service systems.[50] As applied to the legal process, for instance, a defense attorney can use motivational interviewing when working with people who are resistant to court-ordered mental health treatment as a condition of diversion programs. Attorneys can use the technique to guide people through self-identifying benefits of compliance, such as avoiding extended jail time, rejoining their family and community, employment, and other positive life goals. Attorneys can assist people with developing a commitment to change and a commitment to program compliance as a way to achieve the self-identified benefits.

Motivational interviewing is taught through interactive, multi-session courses, including courses tailored specifically to attorneys. There are core concepts that attorneys can apply even in the absence of formal training, but attorneys should seek formal training. The first step to becoming familiar with motivational interviewing basics is understanding the spirit of the approach. Motivational interviewing focuses on collaboration, where practitioners (here, attorneys) are experts in engaging people needing change, and the people are experts on their own lives. Using a strengths-based approach, motivational interviewing recognizes autonomy and self-efficacy, and it appreciates that people have the skills and resources within themselves to bring about change.[51]

Motivational interviewing elicits the language of change through four core skills. Dubbed OARS, these skills encompass open-ended questions, affirmations, reflection, and summation. Rooted in nonjudgment and compassion, motivational interviewing relies on practitioners to draw out information from the people resistant to change. Practitioners use active listening and ask open-ended questions to guide people through considering the benefits of changing and assist them in knowing that change is possible. Practitioners also use affirmations and reflection, such as reaffirming strengths or past attempts toward change, and by expressing empathy through reflective statements. There may be cultural or personal factors that shape how people respond to affirmations. Motivational interviewing includes summarizing what people have said and emphasizing key statements that reinforce their articulated desire

50. Treatment Improvement Protocol 35, *supra* note 47.
51. *Id.*

or commitment to change. Motivational interviewing is goal orientated and recognizes that resolving ambivalence is not always easy. People may express sustain talk, such as expressing the will to maintain the status quo. When there is sustain talk, practitioners should avoid creating a situation that may spark confrontation. Practitioners can approach sustain talk by making reflective statements or by reframing it. This acknowledges people's challenges and concerns, as well as their autonomy. It also assists practitioners in determining how to navigate the conversation to encourage change.[52]

Attorneys who are new to or who already use motivational interviewing can better adapt the approach through key skills and practices. First, attorneys should create a safe and accepting working space to the extent possible.[53] Identify opportunities to ensure that people feel comfortable even in less-than-ideal environments, such as jails or other detention facilities. Learn what is important to people and what may be driving their ambivalence toward change. Identify instances of ambivalence that may require cultural awareness and cultural competence. Avoid forcing people into accepting undesired options if there are opportunities to direct or consider other options.[54] This may not always be possible given the nature of the legal process, particularly if alleged crimes limit charging or disposition options. To illustrate this, a person may want jail time over participation in alternatives to incarceration. If the case is still working its way through the adjudication process, attorneys would discuss all disposition possibilities, including dispositions that may include options for mental health court and community supervision with mental health treatment as a condition of release. Depending on the charge and other circumstances impacting the case, the person may be diverted away from jail and be limited to making decisions about the alternatives to incarceration.

As with any engagement involving reluctance, conversations may slow down or lead to uncomfortable silence. Attorneys should get comfortable with silence. Resist the urge to break the silence to resolve

---

52. *Id.*

53. *Id.*

54. *Id.*

discomfort.[55] Silence that is uncomfortable to attorneys may also be uncomfortable to others. Embracing the silence may lead people to talk more as a way to break their own discomfort. Roll with resistance by working with people to understand and diminish their resistance, and to elicit reasons why they may want to change after all.

Attorneys should identify when there is dissonance between people's behaviors and their values, or dissonance between their behaviors and their stated mental health or criminal justice outcomes. When appropriate, attorneys may benefit from using scaled questions to elicit a willingness to change.[56] Scaled questions can also inform follow-up questions that can help attorneys guide people toward change. For example, attorneys can ask "On a scale of zero to ten, where zero is not confident at all and ten is very confident, how confident are you that you can comply with the treatment requirements of the alternative to incarceration program?" The response to the question can allow attorneys to follow up with questions about why people selected the number and what is needed for them to get to a higher number on the scale.

Incorporating Lawyering Tools to Advance Equity

Trauma-informed lawyering and motivational interviewing embrace the legal theory of therapeutic justice. Therapeutic justice acknowledges the healing power of the law and the impact that legal processes have on psychological well-being. Originally applied to interdisciplinary collaborative courts, therapeutic justice has since expanded to use and acceptance within conventional civil and criminal courts. Similar to procedural justice, therapeutic justice argues that people on all side of the case should receive a sense of value. Therapeutic justice looks at the application of law and reimagines legal processes to improve the legal and life outcomes of people moving through them. Therapeutic justice embraces the principle that law, and the legal process, can positively impact people regardless of

---

55. Olivia Porter, *Better Communication through Motivational Interviewing*, Alt. Disp. Resol. in the Ninth Ct. Newsl. 2 (Spring 2014).

56. Treatment Improvement Protocol 35, *supra* note 47.

case outcome if they are given autonomy and the ability to participate in the legal process. Criminal cases benefiting from therapeutic justice, regardless of case outcome, increase compliance with court orders and the people involved in case are more positively engaged in legal proceedings.[57] Familiarity with trauma-informed lawyering, motivational interviewing, and other promising practices can improve the outcome and experiences for both people moving through the legal process and attorneys.

Tools and Resources

- *State Court Behavioral Health Series* by National Center for State Courts.
- Motivational Interviewing Network of Trainers.
- *Seeing What's Underneath: A Resource for Understanding Behavior and Using Language in Juvenile Court* by the National Juvenile Defender Center, the National Council of Juvenile and Family Court Judges, Fair and Just Prosecution, and the Georgetown Law Juvenile Justice Initiative.
- *Trauma-informed Prosecution Resource* by the Institute for Innovation in Prosecution at John Jay College of Criminal Justice.
- *Trauma-Informed Legal Advocacy: A Resource for Juvenile Defense Attorneys* by the National Child Traumatic Stress Network.
- Bessel Van Der Kolk, The Body Keeps the Score: Brain, Mind, and Body in the Healing of Trauma (Penguin Books 2015).

57. Bruce J. Winick & David B. Wexler, *Drug Treatment Court: Therapeutic Jurisprudence Applied*, 18 Touro Law Rev. 475–89 (2002); Bruce J. Winick & David B. Wexler, *Therapeutic Jurisprudence, in* Principles of Addiction Medicine (Richard K. Ries et al. eds., 4th ed. 2008).

PART III

Equity on Both Sides of the Adversarial System

CHAPTER 5

The Role of Prosecutors in Advancing Equity

The work of prosecutors is far-reaching. Prosecutorial decisions impact more than the people involved in each case. They also impact the community at large. Prosecutors promote the interest of the community and the interest of public safety. They are problem-solvers who seek justice and who consider the broader goals of the criminal justice system. This chapter embraces the role of the prosecutor by first reviewing strategies that prosecutors can take to advance equity when processing cases, followed by a case walkthrough of prosecutorial approaches framed as self-assessment questions to detail key components for leveraging the prosecutor role to evoke change.

Prosecutorial Strategies[1]

The role of prosecutors is not merely to convict. Prosecutors approach cases by exploring what can and should be done within the bounds of the law. They balance judgment by exercising the discretion granted

1. *See generally* Criminal Justice Standards Prosecution Function § 3-1.1 *et seq.* (Am. Bar Ass'n 2017).

to them in pursuing charges when needed and by not pursing charges when appropriate to do so.[2] In approaching cases, prosecutors should look beyond only proving the elements of the crime. Find out why people committed the alleged offense. Look into their motivation or the influences that led to the event. This can provide valuable information about ways to best achieve positive, long-term public safety and public health outcomes. Conducting such an investigation may lead prosecutors to decide on or renew consideration for alternatives to incarceration or inform opportunities to negotiate with defense attorneys about charging or case options that can set people up for success even if incarceration is unavoidable.

Prosecutors should be aware of mental illness, and the influence of mental illness at the time of the alleged offense and the events that led up to it. Prosecutors can use information about the mental illness to inform opportunities to connect people to pre- or post-plea alternatives to incarceration, and as mitigating factors during plea bargaining and when making sentencing recommendations. To field opportunities, prosecutors can consider how prosecution may cause harm to people involved in the case and communities and consider whether the harm outweighs the impacts of prosecution. Examine whether prosecuting the case will inflict collateral consequences, and whether there are other resolutions available that would mitigate their damage.

Public safety is best achieved when people of diverse backgrounds who have mental illness receive access to needed treatment and when they are not interacting with the criminal justice system. This does not always require obtaining a conviction. Sometimes it will be in the interest of the community and public safety to remove people from incarceration settings and connect them to treatment and service in the community. Addressing mental health needs and any other underlying causes that led to criminal justice involvement is often the most effective way for prosecutors to fulfil their duty. When making charging decisions and in processing the case, prosecutors should pursue alternatives to incarceration that avoid further progression though the criminal justice system. Also consider if prosecution will help or hinder people in addressing their

2. *Id.*, Standard 3-1.2(b).

mental illness in the long term. Understand whether a conviction would impact people's ability to be successful upon reentry.

Prosecutors should consider alternatives to incarceration broadly and liberally. These options may be available pre-arrest, pretrial, or in other pre-plea phases, or available post-plea and post-sentence. Consideration for these programs should extend to people who have higher-level charges, as many people facing high-level felony charges can be successful in community-based alternatives. Accessing treatment in the community advances individual health and criminal justice outcomes. It also protects public safety. Treatment in a community setting allows people to access treatment and develop valuable connections in the community where they would be returning following any length of incarceration. Treatment in the community can stabilize them and assist them in addressing their mental health needs and in addressing criminogenic risks and needs that, if left unaddressed, may lead to future justice involvement.

Prosecutors should engage mental health professionals. Mental health professionals who work with people moving through the criminal justice system often share similar perspectives and goals as prosecutors, even if it is not immediately noticeable. Talk with mental health professionals who have experience working with people of diverse backgrounds to get a sense of their approach to treatment, their perspective of the criminal justice system, and how they approach their role in ensuring positive mental health and criminal justice outcomes. Most mental health professionals would agree that they want the people they treat to get stabilized and to change behaviors that will assist them in avoiding future criminal justice involvement. Mental health professionals want justice, and they may view justice differently than prosecutors. Connecting with local mental health professionals can help prosecutors effectively develop case options that satisfy both the pursuit of justice and the pursuit of improved mental health.[3]

---

3. *See generally* David LaBahn et al., *Prosecutor-Led Diversion Programs: Roundtable Discussion*, The Council of State Governments Justice Center & the Bureau of Justice Assistance webinar (Sept. 7, 2021); The Council of State Governments Justice Center, Understanding and Managing Risks for People with Behavioral Health Needs FAQs for Local Prosecutors (Mar. 20, 2021), https://csgjusticecenter.org/wp-content/uploads/2021/03/CSGJC-Prosecutor-FAQ_FINAL508compliant.pdf.

A Guided Self-Assessment for Prosecutors

A challenge prosecutors face in developing a practice centered on equity is moving ideas from aspirational to operational. To meet this challenge, the following self-assessment questions are designed to enhance prosecutorial responses to people of diverse backgrounds who have mental illness. These self-assessment questions walk prosecutors through a series of topics that assess current progress and that identify areas that prosecutors may want to enhance. The self-assessment questions are developed to support continual learning for prosecutors at varying stages of their career—from newly admitted attorneys and attorneys new to prosecution to career prosecutors whose tenures have included cases involving people of diverse backgrounds who have mental illness.

Am I trained on best practices for cases involving people who have mental illness? Am I trained on best practices for cases involving people from diverse and traditionally marginalized backgrounds?

Best practices should encompass evidence-based practices, promising practices, and community-defined practices. Evidence-based practices are strategies that are demonstrated to be effective through empirical research and that have definable and measurable outcomes. Promising practices are strategies that have a potential to lead to positive or improved outcomes and that have been used with success. Community-defined practices are cultural, racial, or traditional practices informed, guided, and determined by a community. Community-defined practices are recognized by community consensus to have positive outcomes.[4]

Training topics should include identification of mental illness and cultural influences on mental illness. Training should focus on attorney interactions with people of diverse backgrounds who have mental illness, including cultural and linguistic competency. Legal training should

4. Ken Martinez et al., *Community-defined Evidence: A Bottom-up Behavioral Health Approach to Measure What Works in Communities of Color*, 10 Emotional & Behav. Disorders in Youth 11–16 (2010).

be incorporated into daily practice and should include legal protections, alternatives to incarceration, and other available disposition options.

Am I continually learning about the lived experiences of people involved in the criminal justice system who have mental illness, including those from diverse backgrounds?

Gaining awareness of lived experiences can involve attending training hosted by local providers and advocacy groups, engaging peer groups, touring social service provider facilities, or having candid conversations with people who have exited the criminal justice system and who are willing to share their experiences. Knowledge of social determinates of mental health can assist attorneys in recognizing opportunities to advance this learning. Social determinates of mental health that remain unaddressed can increase the likelihood of repeat criminal justice involvement. Social determinants of mental health identify areas where attorneys can learn more, and can highlight determinants where it may be useful to engage culturally responsive service providers.

Am I aware of mental health treatment, wrap-around services, and other resources that serve the various neighborhoods and communities within my jurisdiction?

Treatment and services should engage diverse populations and be culturally responsive. Be familiar with service providers that have representative staff that share cultural identities with people referred, as well as providers that have proven experience serving people of various backgrounds. Providers should have experience treating people involved in the criminal justice system. If possible, make in-person visits and tours with each provider. In-person visits should extend to court-ordered services and services that people may seek out voluntarily following referral from prosecutors. In-person visits allow attorneys to gain a better understanding of what it is like for people to seek and receive services from each provider. Explore the extent to which mental health treatment providers are willing to integrate people's beliefs, practices, identity and cultural backgrounds into treatment and case plans.

Wrap-around services offer resources that address unmet social needs that may indirectly impact mental illness and may indirectly increase the likelihood of criminal justice involvement. Wrap-around service providers can include legal aid organizations, housing providers, employment services, and reentry service providers. Explore the extent to which wraparound providers are willing to integrate people's beliefs, practices, identity, and cultural backgrounds into services provided.

Am I regularly engaging with other prosecutors, defense attorneys, and criminal justice professionals to improve policies and procedures that impact people of diverse backgrounds who have mental illness?

Explore available opportunities to network and build relationships with other criminal justice professionals. Harnessing these relationships can create openings to advance equity through the prosecutor role, such as through improved case coordination and processing. Prosecutors who hold policymaking roles have opportunities to leverage their position to assess agency policies and procedures and to influence change. Policymakers should explore opportunities to revisit agency policies influencing charging guidelines, admittance into alternatives to incarceration and diversion programs, and other policies that can protect the public while connecting people to treatment and services that allow for positive, long-term justice outcomes. Leveraging the policymaking role may extend to impacting the broader criminal justice system. This may include participation on criminal justice coordinating councils or similar venues that bring together key criminal justice professionals to improve criminal justice responses.

When I screen a case, how do I know when a person has a mental illness?

Examine factors that prosecutors commonly look for when identifying mental illness and ensure the factors correctly identify people. Examine behaviors, results from mental health screens, or other criteria. Assess the extent to which these factors may vary based on race, culture, or other influences. Evaluate the rate at which these factors have successfully allowed prosecutors to identify mental illness among people of varying races and cultures. Determine whether factors used to identify mental illness disproportionately identify or disproportionately overlook certain races or people from certain communities. Examine whether factors used to identify mental illness may contribute to inconsistent results. Decide whether additional cultural or equity education is needed.

Do I consider mental health needs through an equity lens when reviewing cases and determining a charging level?

Review all factors that influence whether to file cases and, if filed, the charging level. Appreciate that conviction may not be in the best interest of the public and the community to which the people facing criminal charges will return. Most people are better served through mental health systems than through criminal justice systems, and mental health treatment may more effectively deter behaviors leading to future criminal justice involvement. Avoid compounding charges as a negotiation tactic for plea bargaining. Pursue opportunities that mitigate inequities. Consider whether the people whose alleged crimes teeter between higher and lower charges will attain better long-term criminal justice and health outcomes if convicted on lower charges. Explore and mitigate unintended influences on decision-making. Identify influences such as subjectivity among decision-makers, subjectivity in eligibility criteria for various disposition options, and implications resulting from racially or culturally neutral screening and assessment tools.

Have I approached cases involving people of diverse backgrounds who have mental illness through an equity lens when making disposition decisions and sentencing recommendations?

Disposition options may include dismissal, pre-plea diversion, pre- and post-plea alternatives to incarceration, or conviction with jail or prison time. Identify situations where decision-making should consider mental illness and situations where mental illness should not be a factor. Measure the extent to which disposition options are equitable across people of diverse backgrounds. Identify factors that may limit equitable referrals to alternatives to incarceration. Pursue opportunities where prosecutors can directly address these factors.

Have I considered mental health and cultural factors at other decision points, such as determining bail or pretrial release, conditions of release, and so on?

Examine whether race or the presence of a mental illness influences bail or release recommendations, and whether those factors influence determinations made by decision-makers. Identify situations where decision-makers do not consider these factors but should, and identify situations where decision-makers do consider these factors but the factors should not play a role in decision-making. Recommendations about conditions of release should go beyond a uniform set of conditions for anyone who has mental illness. Instead, individually tailor recommended conditions to maximize the likelihood of compliance and success.

Connect people to mental health treatment or wraparound services only when appropriate to do so, and examine due process considerations when making recommendations. Determine what, if any, conditions are reasonable, culturally appropriate, and feasible based on individual circumstances. Prioritize more restrictive conditions and required treatment for people with the highest criminogenic risks and needs. Lower-risk people can often correct criminal behaviors and return to court without court involvement. Overtaxing low- and medium-risk people with conditions to release can directly cause negative criminal justice outcomes.[5] Medical necessity should dictate conditions requiring mental health treatment, as determined by a licensed mental health professional who has a proven history of making culturally appropriate determinations.

---

5. *See, e.g.*, Douglas B. Marlow, *The Most Carefully Studied, yet Least Understood, Terms in the Criminal Justice Lexicon: Risk, Need, and Responsivity*, Policy Research Associates, https://www.prainc.com/risk-need-responsitivity (last visited Mar. 27, 2022); National Institutes of Correction, Module 5: Section 2. The Risk-Need-Responsivity Model for Assessment and Rehabilitation, https://info.nicic.gov/tjc/module-5-section-2-risk-need-responsivity-model-assessment-and-rehabilitation (last visited Mar. 27, 2022).

Only make conditions requiring treatment if treatment is available and accessible. Consider individual factors such as transportation, financial ability, and other factors that can influence access to treatment and treatment compliance.

Do I negotiate with defense attorneys through an equity lens?

Preparing for negotiations should include understanding the impact the case will have on the people involved, any survivors of crime, the community, and the public at large. Appreciate that serving the public and ensuring public safety may entail dismissal of charges or connecting people to treatment in the community in lieu of incarceration. Recognize collateral consequences of conviction, particularly those amplified for people of diverse backgrounds. Understand the extent to which disposition options may advance or interrupt positive health and criminal justice outcomes. Certain disposition options may cause harm by disconnecting people from existing mental health treatment or causing them to lose public health benefits such as Medicaid, Social Security Disability Insurance (SSDI), or Supplemental Security Income (SSI). Avoidable incarceration can also cause harm by causing people to lose employment, lose housing, lose placement in housing voucher programs, and so on. These losses amplify socioeconomic inequities experienced by people of diverse backgrounds and people from traditionally marginalized backgrounds.

Am I advocating that the person receives mental health treatment or medication while in custody?

Prosecutors should ensure people in need of treatment receive medically appropriate treatment in a timely and responsive manner while housed in jail or prison. Understand cultural impacts in the expression of mental illness and associated behaviors. Correctional staff, custodial medical providers, and other custody personnel commonly misidentify behaviors and expressions indicative of mental illness due to cultural misunderstandings, misperceptions, prejudices, and biases. Refer people exhibiting behaviors symptomatic of a mental illness for assessment. Prosecutors should tour detention facilities used by their jurisdiction. Visit jails, prisons, locked mental health facilities, and other facilities used to house people moving through the criminal justice system. These tours provide opportunities to observe the experiences of people housed therein and to understand treatment settings. Examine whether detention facilities impose fees for the provision of medical treatment or medication, such as medical copayments. Medical copayments can create an added barrier to access for most people in jail and prison. Medical copayments can also exacerbate economic inequities, particularly among people of diverse backgrounds and people from traditionally marginalized communities.

Tools and Resources

- *My Community Resources Checklist to Identify Local Treatment and Supports* by the Judges and Psychiatrists Leadership Initiative.
- *Judges' Guide to Mental Illnesses in the Courtroom* by the Judges and Psychiatrists Leadership Initiative.
- *Procedural Justice* by the Justice Collaboratory at Yale Law School.

CHAPTER 6

The Role of Defense Attorneys in Advancing Equity

The role of defense attorneys in representing people of diverse backgrounds who have mental illness is to provide advocacy. For defense attorneys to be effective, they must build trusting relationships. This means creating a balance between professionalism and compassion and ensuring that people are afforded the highest quality of advocacy. This chapter embraces the role of defense attorneys by first reviewing strategies that attorneys can take to advance equity through representation and advocacy. It is followed by a case walkthrough framed as self-assessment questions to detail key components for leveraging the defense attorney role to evoke change.

Representation and Advocacy[1]

Defense attorneys have an ethical obligation to provide effective representation. This involves individualizing responses to each case to avoid adopting a one-size-fits-all approach to representation. Communication

1. *See generally* Criminal Justice Standards Defense Function § 4-1.1 *et seq.* (Am. Bar Ass'n 2017).

and decision-making styles that worked with one person may not work for others, even if case characteristics and client racial or sociocultural backgrounds are similar. Be adaptive and flexible. Embrace innovation when providing advocacy.

Advocacy includes guiding the dialog around how the mental illness has affected the case. Be strategic in advising clients whether to raise mental illness as part of the case, and discuss any advantages or disadvantages of doing so. Be mindful when advising people about whether to seek mental health treatment, and be open to any concerns or disagreements they may have. Effective representation involves more than simply advising clients. Defense attorneys must build cases that pursue all available legal actions and that provide the best possible outcome. Be strategic in making motions, and be creative when working with opposing counsel to develop case dispositions. Consider opportunities that lead to medically and culturally responsive treatment and services that attend to social and criminogenic needs.

Recognize that sometimes the advocacy role means inviting mental health professionals to advocate. Mental health advocacy can help paint a picture of people's unmet mental health needs. These unmet needs play a role in the lead up to the alleged offenses, and they should be considered when thinking through case strategy. This can help focus attention about mental illness away from stigmatizing assumptions, such as assumptions that people who have mental illness—particularly those of diverse backgrounds—are inherently dangerous, broken, or criminal. Focus the case on what happened to them and what needs to be addressed to achieve therapeutic justice outcomes.

A Guided Self-Assessment for Defense Attorneys

A challenge defense attorneys may face in developing a practice centered on advancing equity is moving ideas from aspirational to operational. To meet this challenge, the following self-assessment questions are designed to enhance advocacy for people of diverse backgrounds who have mental illness. The self-assessment questions walk defense attorneys through a series of topics to assess current progress and to identify areas that attorneys may want to enhance. The self-assessment questions are developed to support continual learning for defense attorneys at varying stages of their career—from newly admitted attorneys and attorneys new to criminal defense to career defense attorneys whose tenures have involved advocating for people of diverse backgrounds who have mental illness.

Am I trained on best practices for cases involving people who have mental illness? Am I trained on best practices for cases involving people from diverse and traditionally marginalized backgrounds?

Best practices should encompass evidence-based practices, promising practices, and community-defined practices. Evidence-based practices are strategies that are demonstrated to be effective through empirical research and that have definable and measurable outcomes. Promising practices are strategies that have a potential to lead to positive or improved outcomes and that have been used with success. Community-defined practices are cultural, racial, or traditional practices informed, guided, and determined by a community. Community-defined practices are recognized by community consensus to have positive outcomes.[2]

Training topics should include identification of mental illness and cultural influences on mental illness. Training should focus on attorney interactions with people of diverse backgrounds who have mental illness, including cultural and linguistic competency. Legal training should be incorporated into daily practice and should include legal protections, alternatives to incarceration, and other available disposition options.

Am I continually learning about the lived experiences of people involved in the criminal justice system who have mental illness, including those from diverse backgrounds?

Gaining awareness of lived experiences can involve attending training hosted by local providers and advocacy groups, engaging peer groups,

2. Ken Martinez et al., *Community-defined Evidence: A Bottom-up Behavioral Health Approach to Measure What Works in Communities of Color*, 10 Emotional & Behav. Disorders in Youth 11–16 (2010).

touring social service provider facilities, or having candid conversations with people who have exited the criminal justice system and who are willing to share their experiences. Knowledge of social determinates of mental health can assist attorneys in recognizing opportunities to advance this learning. Social determinates of mental health that remain unaddressed can increase the likelihood of repeat criminal justice involvement. Social determinants of mental health identify areas where attorneys can learn more and can highlight determinants where it may be useful to engage culturally responsive service providers.

Am I aware of mental health treatment, wrap-around services, and other resources that serve the various neighborhoods and communities within my jurisdiction?

Treatment and services should engage diverse populations and be culturally responsive. Be familiar with service providers that have representative staff that share cultural identities with people referred, as well as providers that have proven experience serving people of various backgrounds. Providers should have experience treating people involved in the criminal justice system. If possible, make in-person visits and tours with each provider. In-person visits should extend to court-ordered services and services that people may seek out voluntarily following referral from defense attorneys. In-person visits allow attorneys to gain a better understanding of what it is like for people to seek and receive services from each provider. Explore the extent to which mental health treatment providers are willing to integrate people's beliefs, practices, identity, and cultural backgrounds into treatment and case plans.

Wrap-around services offer resources that address unmet social needs that may indirectly impact mental illness and may indirectly increase the likelihood of criminal justice involvement. Wrap-around service providers can include legal aid organizations, housing providers, employment services, and reentry service providers. Explore the extent to which wraparound providers are willing to integrate people's beliefs, practices, identity, and cultural backgrounds into services provided.

Do I understand the consequential intricacies of accessing public benefits, mental health treatment, and wraparound services? Do I recognize how these intricacies may inform negotiations or other opportunities to advocate for my client?

Be familiar with timelines and processes associated with public benefits, mental health treatment, and wraparound services. Be aware of timelines and processes that may be jeopardized if certain disposition options are pursued, or if specified protocols are not followed. Recognize the ways in which various disposition options can affect those timelines and processes, including disposition options that may interrupt eligibility or qualification criteria. For instance, placement on a housing voucher waiting list may be jeopardized if people lose their "homelessness" status due to extended incarceration at pretrial or post-sentence stages.

Access to public benefits may involve certain elements that require strategic planning when it comes to people moving through the criminal justice system. Public benefits may be an important reentry need for people from traditionally marginalized communities or people who are indigent. Access to public mental health benefits may require careful negotiation to ensure court-ordered treatment meets statutorily required medical necessity criteria. Access to financial and public food assistance programs following exit from the criminal justice system, for instance, may encourage defense attorneys to purse disposition options that will allow people opportunities to meet work credit requirements.

Am I regularly engaging with other defense attorneys, prosecutors, and criminal justice professionals to improve policies and procedures that impact people of diverse backgrounds who have mental illness?

Explore available opportunities to network and build relationships with other criminal justice professionals. Harnessing these relationships can create openings to advance equity through the defense attorney role, such as through improved case coordination and processing. Defense attorneys who hold policymaking roles have opportunities to leverage their position to assess agency policies and procedures and to influence change. Leveraging the policymaking role may extend to impacting the broader criminal justice system. This may include participation on criminal justice coordinating councils or similar venues that bring together key criminal justice professionals to improve criminal justice responses.

Regardless of policymaking capacity or rank, this engagement should include working with the court, prosecutors, and other decision-makers to ensure everyone involved in a case has foundational knowledge about mental illness and cultural influences that will lead to the best possible health and criminal justice outcomes. This includes educating decision-makers on the impact that various disposition options will have on health and justice outcomes, including recidivism, as well as the impact that disposition options will have on witnesses and on the community. Education should seek to mitigate stigma or bias that decision-makers may carry about people of diverse backgrounds or mental illness.

Inform decision-makers about the impact that incarceration has on mental illness, including research about the impacts that different carceral settings have on people of diverse backgrounds who have mental illness. If alternatives to incarceration and diversion options are available, educate decision-makers on research and other persuasive information about the positive impacts of those programs on people of diverse backgrounds. Provide information about the impact of culturally appropriate mental health treatment in improving responsivity.

When I meet clients, how do I learn about their mental health history?

Ask people about their mental health history and conduct a separate investigation about their history. Investigation may include receiving collateral information, such as mental health records from treatment received in the community or in the jail, information about previous hospitalizations, or past involvement in the competence to stand trial process. Pay particular attention and care when representing people who are immigrants, regardless of immigration status. Determine whether medical history is obtainable from the other countries in which people have lived and if there are other mechanisms for verifying mental health history. Practice mindful communication when addressing situations where people fail to disclose their mental health history. Approaching the situation prudently builds trust and improves future conversations about their mental health needs.

Learn about processes for referring people for mental health screens or assessments upon booking into jail or at other criminal justice decision points. As cultural misunderstandings and structural inequities can limit access to mental health treatment in community and in carceral settings, people of diverse backgrounds are disproportionately misidentified as not having a mental illness even when screened in jail. Refer people for a mental health evaluation any time their behavior or other factors suggest a mental or behavioral health need.

When I meet clients, how do I learn about the totality of their circumstances?

Ask questions that capture an array of factors that impact people's lives, the case at hand, and long-term health and criminal justice goals. Questions should encompass factors that contributed to their current justice involvement and factors to address when moving the case forward to prevent future justice involvement. Factors should denote social determinants of mental health, including health and access to health care, housing stability, economic stability, and family and social community. Defense attorneys should gather information in a responsive and empathetic manner. Depending on available resources, address unmet mental health and social needs while the case is pending and once the case is dismissed or adjudicated. This can be done through the direct attorney-client relationship, if appropriate, or through other available mechanisms. Make referrals to social workers, social service agencies, and legal agencies. Referrals should be mindful of people's mental health and cultural backgrounds. Refer people to providers who have experience working with people involved in the criminal justice system, people who have mental illness, and people of diverse backgrounds. Ensure that referred providers are willing to integrate people's beliefs, practices, identity, and cultural backgrounds into treatment and case plans.

When I meet clients, how do I learn about their culture and the cultural etiquettes that would be valuable in zealously advocating for them?

Avoid making blanket assumptions about people's race, ethnicity, nationality, and other perceivable characteristics that draw conclusions about their identity and culture. Do not assume that people share etiquettes or practices based solely on their physical identity. Avoid assumptions that people share the attorney's culture and cultural etiquettes, and avoid assumptions that people share the cultural etiquettes of past clients of similar backgrounds. People within any race or culture have intersectional identities and experiences. Take time to understand attitudes, beliefs, and behaviors that are important to them. Different cultures may have varying approaches and beliefs about mental illness and criminal justice involvement. Some cultures may consider discussing mental illness outside of medical or personal relationships as taboo. Some cultures may stigmatize mental illness or criminal justice involvement. Attorneys should tailor their approaches to ensure representation and advocacy are culturally appropriate and mindful of cultural considerations around mental illness.

Ask open-ended questions about people's race, ethnicity, culture, and other characteristics that are important to them. Ask people directly about how they wish to be identified, and about their cultural norms and expectations. Observe their body language and behaviors. Some cultures, for instance, may avoid making eye contact when speaking with unfamiliar people or people in positions of power or authority.

Appreciate that legal and courtroom decorum and customs are not a default. People may be unfamiliar with courtroom decorum, even if they have previously gone through the legal process. Discuss courtroom decorum and other expectations that will be placed on them when they appear in front of judges, jurors, or other decision-makers. Identify behaviors that may be misconstrued by decision-makers, including behaviors expressing culture and behaviors rooted in mental illness and trauma. Develop a plan of action to ensure behaviors rooted in mental illness and trauma are not met with stigma or bias. Engage people in respectful conversations about behaviors that express culture and listen to their questions. Collaborate with them to determine ways to best move forward to ensure decision-makers afford them objectivity while enabling them to authentically express themselves and their culture.

Am I asking my client questions to understand whether their current or past interactions within the criminal justice system included behaviors indicative of mental illness?

Consider whether behaviors indicative of mental illness or behavioral health conditions may have been overlooked or misinterpreted. Past health conditions that were unidentified or ignored may lend to case strategy. Examine whether implicit or explicit biases, stigmas, or cultural misunderstandings may have been a factor. This may include past interactions with the criminal justice system involving co-occurring disorders where illicit drug use or possession was identified but mental illness was not. People who have mental illness are likely to become justice involved due to substance use arising out of self-medication for a mental illness, as well as mental illness induced by substance use. This encompasses instances where mental illness remains undiagnosed, unidentified, or otherwise not a factor in criminal cases.

Am I working with my client to examine all potential benefits, and risks, of addressing their mental illness as part of the case?

Examine the impacts of raising mental illness as part of a case, including impacts that can carry over once people exit the criminal justice system. Discuss benefits and risks associated with each disposition option, and discuss the benefits and risks of raising mental illness as a mitigating factor or defense. Assess the extent to which cultural differences, language differences, and socioeconomic factors may impact the case. Analyze these factors and discuss whether to raise mental illness as part of the defense in light of them. Pay attention to questions and concerns that people have. Listen to their concerns about cultural stigmas around mental illness, impacts that may arise if a mental illness is disclosed in a public manner, and experience-based mistrust of or hesitancies about mental health treatment in community or carceral settings.

Am I knowledgeable about the competence to stand trial and restoration processes?

Recognize when competence to stand trial processes would be appropriate, and when it would be inappropriate to raise doubt. Compare the differences between competency restoration services and mental health treatment. The competence to stand trial and restoration processes are not a pathway to ongoing, long-term mental health treatment and services. Recognize occasions where declaring doubt could be a matter of cultural misunderstanding that could be effectively addressed through other procedural vehicles. This can involve language or linguistic misunderstandings, misinterpretations of cultural expression or behaviors, or challenges rooted in fear or experience-based mistrust of attorneys or of the criminal justice system.

Am I zealously advocating for alternatives to incarceration or other dispositions that would connect my client to treatment in the community?

Ensure that treatment or programs in which people are connected are medically and culturally responsive. Treatment and programs should maximize the likelihood of treatment compliance and should promote positive mental health and criminal justice outcomes. Evaluate whether any treatment options may create disparate impacts, including sociocultural or socioeconomic impacts. A court-ordered program, for instance, may require a residential component that is located in an unfamiliar or culturally dissimilar neighborhood, or the program may utilize different cultural etiquettes or courtesies. Advocate for programs that will integrate people's beliefs, practices, identity, and cultural backgrounds into treatment plans.

Am I advocating for my client to receive mental health treatment or medication while in custody?

Defense attorneys should ensure people in need of treatment receive medically appropriate treatment while housed in jail or prison in a timely and responsive manner. Understand cultural impacts in the expression of mental illness and associated behaviors. Correctional staff, custodial medical providers, and other custody personnel commonly misidentify behaviors and expressions indicative of mental illness due to cultural misunderstandings, misperceptions, prejudices, and biases. Refer people exhibiting behaviors symptomatic of a mental illness for assessment.

Defense attorneys should tour detention facilities used by their jurisdiction. Visit jails, prisons, locked mental health facilities, and other facilities used to house people moving through the criminal justice system. These tours provide opportunities to observe the experiences of people housed therein and to understand treatment settings. Investigate whether criminal or civil law procedures may apply to clients' individual circumstances, such as petitioning for or advocating against voluntary or involuntary medication orders while in custody pretrial or post-conviction. Examine whether detention facilities impose fees for the provision of medical treatment or medication, such as medical copayments. Medical copayments can create an added barrier to access for most people in jail and prison. Medical copayments can also exacerbate economic inequities, particularly among people of diverse backgrounds and people from traditionally marginalized communities.

Have I advocated for connections in mental health treatment upon release from incarceration?

Advocate for connections to treatment and services at all stage of release. Release can take place at many stages along the criminal justice continuum, including pretrial release, release to alternatives to incarceration, release upon dismissal of charges, post-sentence release, and release from court-ordered community supervision. Mental health treatment and services should be medically appropriate and culturally responsive. Defense attorneys should ensure that connections to treatment and services will set people up for success. Connections to treatment and services should be mindful of integrating people's beliefs, practices, identity, and cultural backgrounds into treatment and case plans. Advocate for people to be released during daytime hours when treatment and services are open for business. Advocate for other immediate concerns that are important to address, such as release options that enable people to access to transportation or other immediate supports.

Tools and Resources

- *My Community Resources Checklist to Identify Local Treatment and Supports* by the Judges and Psychiatrists Leadership Initiative.
- *Judges' Guide to Mental Illnesses in the Courtroom* by the Judges and Psychiatrists Leadership Initiative.
- Representing People with Mental Disabilities: A Criminal Defense Lawyer's Best Practices Manual (Elizabeth Kelley ed., American Bar Association 2018).
- *Procedural Justice* by the Justice Collaboratory at Yale Law School.

PART IV

Advancing Equity across the Criminal Justice Continuum

CHAPTER 7

Initial Criminal Justice Involvement and Pre-Adjudication

People of diverse backgrounds who have mental illness often become involved in the criminal justice system. They become involved as the people accused of crime, or as witnesses or survivors of crime. Involvement in the criminal justice system is a function of bias. Consider that, for many, involvement is not a predictor of criminality or dangerousness but, rather, is a result of inequity. This chapter begins the conversation about opportunities along the criminal justice continuum where attorneys can use their role to advance equity for those who become justice involved.

The concept of procedural justice is important to this conversation. Procedural justice plays a role in the progression of cases through the legal process and the way people perceive fairness and justice. When people feel a sense of procedural justice, they are more likely to comply with court orders and less likely to engage in future criminal activity.[1] People

1. Fair and Just Prosecution, Issues at a Glance, Building Community Trust Procedural Justice: Enhancing the Legitimacy of the Justice System, https://www.fairandjustprosecution.org/staging/wp-content/uploads/2017/09/FJPBrief.ProceduralJustice.9.25.pdf (last visited Mar. 27, 2022).

of diverse backgrounds who have mental illness can experience events that can build up or destroy their sense of procedural justice. Consider case processing delays. Delays can negatively impact procedural justice and negatively impact symptoms of mental illness. Spending hours going to and from court appearances that do not move cases toward resolution, and waiting weeks between court appearances, can diminish procedural justice and can exacerbate unmet mental health needs and cause decompensation.[2]

With an eye toward procedural justice, this chapter details opportunities that attorneys can pursue at crucial decision points. While this chapter recognizes that mental health care improves reentry success and reduces recidivism,[3] keep in mind certain dynamics that factor into mental health treatment and people's decisions to engage in services:

- The decision to engage in mental health treatment is that of each person. People may be receptive to treatment or refuse it. People may refuse treatment even if it is court ordered. While attorneys cannot force people to engage in mental health treatment, motivational interviewing can help guide conversations in the direction of voluntary treatment compliance when negotiating disposition options.[4]
- Responsivity is a key part of reducing future criminal behavior and reducing recidivism. Numerous factors can influence responsivity, including cultural responsiveness and mental health stability. It is helpful to first address responsivity before addressing criminal behavior and circumstances that drive it. Medication compliance is often an important component leading to responsivity, as is cultural competency and cultural awareness. Medication compliance may stabilize mental illness, and, without stabilization, people

2. The Council of State Governments Justice Center & National Center for State Courts, Improving Case Processing and Outcomes for People with Behavioral Health Needs (Feb. 2021), https://csgjusticecenter.org/wp-content/uploads/2021/02/Accessible_Improving-Case-Processing.pdf.

3. Nathan W. Link et al., *Consequences of Mental and Physical Health for Reentry and Recidivism: Toward a Health-based Model of Desistance,* 57 Criminology 544 (2019).

4. *See* Chapter 4: *Establishing Lawyering Tools for Advancing Equity.*

may engage in repeat or new behaviors that trigger criminal justice responses.

- Finally, stabilization is not always linear. People who have mental illness may experience long-term, recurring symptoms. It is possible, however, to manage the severity and frequency of symptoms and episodes to reduce the likelihood of future criminal behavior and recidivism.

The following glance across the criminal justice continuum covers significant stages of the criminal justice system and legal process prior to case resolution. It focuses on people charged with crimes. The following chapter continues this focus and explores criminal justice system and legal processes following adjudication and the consequences of criminal justice involvement. Later on, a full chapter is dedicated to special considerations for witnesses and survivors of crime.

Pre-Arrest and Pre-Booking Diversion

Many jurisdictions are diverting people who have mental illness away from jail by implementing programs early in the criminal justice system to reduce the number of avoidable arrests. These diversion programs connect people to treatment and services in the community instead of moving them through the legal process. Diversion programs emerging nationwide comprise of pre-booking or pre-charge diversion, expanded cite and release programs, police and mental health co-responder programs, and other innovative programs that provide rehabilitative support. These programs consider the circumstances surrounding alleged offenses and consider people's unmet mental health and social needs. Diversion programs go a long way in reducing arrests when criminalization can be avoided.

Attorneys have the ability and, arguably, the responsibility to ensure that entry into pre-arrest and pre-booking diversion programs is equitable. People of diverse backgrounds who have mental illness can be overlooked for diversion programs due to factors such as false assumptions about their dangerousness. People who have mental illness are falsely assumed to be at high risk of violence and to pose a threat to public safety,[5] and this is amplified for people of diverse backgrounds.[6] Attorneys should examine program admission and investigate admission criteria or other decision-making that rely on subjective determinations of law enforcement and other referrers. Explore whether diversion program admissions are equitable across local populations or whether programs favor or overlook certain people. Additionally, review considerations associated with diversion programs that may impact the case at hand or impact the role of attorneys should there be a need for prosecution.

Arrest and Booking

Appreciating the perspectives of people moving through the arrest and booking processes allows attorneys to determine whether they need to take specific actions to ensure justice. People of diverse backgrounds who have mental illness may have unique experiences that impose crucial and inadvertent consequences on cases. Engaging with law enforcement during arrest or booking is stressful for anyone and creates a heightened level of duress for people of diverse backgrounds who have mental illness. Duress can lead to decompensation, hiding one's mental illness, or conforming behavior to please authority figures. People may exercise passive compliance and passive obedience. This can be a result of structural and historical inequities, mental illness or trauma responses, or experience-based fear of law enforcement.

Conduct a comprehensive investigation into circumstances surrounding arrest. Conduct a holistic investigation that looks at the whole

---

5. Leading research shows that only 3 to 5 percent of violent acts committed in the United States of America can be attributed to people who have serious mental illness. *Mental Health Myths and Facts*, U.S. Dep't of Health & Human Serv. (2022), https://www.mentalhealth.gov/basics/mental-health-myths-facts (last visited June 7, 2022). *See also* Chelsea Halle et al., *The Link between Mental Health, Crime and Violence*, 58 New Ideas in Psych. (2020); Ghiasi, Noman et al., *Psychiatric Illness and Criminality*, StatPearls (Jan. 2021), https://www.ncbi.nlm.nih.gov/books/NBK537064/ (last visited Mar. 27, 2022); Jefferey W. Swanson et al., *Mental Illness and Reduction of Gun Violence and Suicide: Bringing Epidemiologic Research to Policy*, 25 Annals of Epidemiology 366 (2014).

6. *See, e.g.*, Jennifer L. Eberhardt et al., *Seeing Black: Race, Crime, and Visual Processing*, 87 J Personality & Social Psych. 876 (2004) ("The stereotype of Black Americans as violent and criminal has been documented by social psychologists for almost 60 years.").

person and considers social and psychological factors that impacted them. Through a sequential approach, look at activities surrounding the arrest and determine whether subjective or other improper influences were involved. This can involve cultural misunderstandings or stigmas expressed by responding and arresting officers. These expressions can manifest through verbal communication, physical action, physical inaction, or communication in police reports. These expressions can encompass misinterpreting facts or incomplete information gathering.

Common examples of stigma and bias during arrests focus on overt expressions of racism, sexism, homophobia, or nationalism. Officer bias, however, can also result from non-obvious causes. Bias and other misunderstandings can result from lack of experience working with certain racial groups or communities, or from lack of experience responding to certain calls for service.[7] It may be the first time that law enforcement officers, for example, respond to calls for service involving people who have mental illness or people of certain backgrounds. Officers may be inexperienced in defusing situations involving people experiencing psychotic episodes or drug-induced psychoses. Bias can also arise when officers respond to frequent utilizers of jails, emergency departments, and other public systems. Officers who have experience responding to calls for service involving repeat parties can develop bias toward those parties,[8] particularly if the parties continually engage in similar behaviors or similar offenses.

Attorneys should investigate events that take place during arrest and booking to determine whether there is a need for legal intervention. Among other factors, focus investigation on the following matters:

- May the biases, cultural misunderstandings, or stigmas held by arresting officers or other responding officers impact the case?
- Was mental illness identified during arrest or booking? If so, will the methods used to identify mental illness impact the case?

---

7. Trauma Informed Prosecution Presentation, Institute for Innovation in Prosecution at John Jay College of Criminal Justice, https://www.prosecution.org/s/IIP-Trauma-Informed-Prosecution.pptx (last visited Mar. 27, 2022).
8. *Id.*

- May the biases, cultural misunderstandings, or stigmas held by responding medical professionals in the community or in detention facilities impact the case?
- Are there structural inequities embedded in policies, procedures, or tools of the trade? If so, how may they impact the case? Do any of these elements reproduce inequities or disparities?

Law Enforcement Interview and Interrogation

Law enforcement interview and interrogation is a significant stage worthy of attorney investigation. Interrogation techniques can reflect officer stigma, bias, and cultural misunderstandings. Furthermore, techniques that are typically allowable may be deceptive when used with people who have mental illness. Attorneys should explore behaviors exhibited by both interviewers and interviewees during these stages to understand what impacts, if any, behaviors have on the case. It is easy to picture scenarios where mental illness causes uncooperativeness or unresponsiveness, limits comprehension of the actions taking place, or escalates or prolongs these events. Beyond these obvious scenarios, people of diverse backgrounds who have a mental illness may exhibit behaviors warranting careful review.

Consider false confessions. People who have mental illness and people of diverse backgrounds have high rates of false confession.[9] This presents an area ripe for attorney investigation. Mental illness and trauma responses may cause people to pretend to understand their rights when, in actuality, they do not. People of diverse backgrounds who have mental illness may misinterpret the voluntariness of their statements and experience reactions that make them prone to false and uncounseled

---

9. *See, e.g.*, Melanie Clark Mogavero, *An Exploratory Examination of Intellectual Disability and Mental Illness Associated with Alleged False Confessions*, 13 Behav. Sci. & L. 299–316 (2020); Allison D. Redlich, *Law & Psychiatry: Mental Illness, Police Interrogations, and the Potential for False Confession*, Psychiatry Online (Jan. 1, 2004), https://ps.psychiatryonline.org/doi/full/10.1176/appi.ps.55.1.19; Samuel R. Gross et al., *Race and Wrongful Convictions in the United States*, National Registry of Exonerations (2017).

statements.[10] Reactions can include experiencing duress, fear of authority figures, or manifestations of mental illness and trauma.[11]

Attorneys should investigate whether people understood their rights and had the mental capacity to waive rights intelligently and voluntarily. Identify cultural dynamics and misunderstandings that may impact people's ability to act in a voluntary and informed capacity. Determine whether law enforcement conduct could be coercive when directed toward people who have mental illness, even if conduct would not be coercive when directed toward people without mental illness. Such situations may invalidate the voluntariness of statements. Examine the reliability of uncounseled statements and determine any necessary countermeasures to mitigate the impact that statements have on the case or determine what countermeasures are necessary.

Mental illness and trauma can affect memory, awareness, perception, and other mental processes that can alter one's ability to remember facts correctly, make decisions, and exercise sound judgment and reasoning. This can lead to coerced-compliant false confessions, particularly for people who feel as though they are under duress and want to avoid the stress of interrogation. Mental illness can lead to coerced-internalized false confessions in people subject to deceptive interrogation techniques. This is particularly the case for people who begin to believe, based on the suggestions of law enforcement, that they committed the crime even if they did not commit the crime or have no recollection of the events relayed to them during the interrogation. Mental illness can also lead to voluntary false confessions, particularly if the severity of mental illness restricts one's ability to appreciate the gravity of the situation.[12] Unless the court finds the use of impermissible coercive conduct during interrogation, the false statements made due to mental illness, trauma, fear, or duress may not be excluded from evidence.

---

10. *See, e.g.*, *False Confessions & Recording of Custodial Interrogations*, The Innocence Project https://innocenceproject.org/false-confessions-recording-interrogations/ (last visited Mar. 27, 2022).

11. Saul M. Kassin, *False Confessions Causes, Consequences, and Implications for Reform*, Current Directions Psychological Sci. 249, 251 (2008).

12. Alexis E. Carl, *Dead Wrong: Capital Punishment, Wrongful Convictions, and Serious Mental Illness*, 1 Wrongful Conviction L. Rev. 336–63 (2020) [hereinafter *Dead Wrong*].

Attorneys can recognize signs that people may have made false confessions or are at risk of doing so. Signs of mental illness and other heightened behaviors can be a sign of false confession. High anxiety, risky or reckless behaviors, uncommonly high or low self-esteem, uncommonly high or low assertiveness, memory deficiency, and delusional behavior can be indicators of specific mental health conditions that mark proneness for false confessions.[13] People experiencing high anxiety may be at risk of coerced-compliant false confessions. People exhibiting reckless behaviors, or uncommonly high or low self-esteem or assertiveness, may be at risk of making voluntary false confessions. People experiencing memory deficiencies or delusions may be at risk of making coerced-internalized false confessions.[14]

Attorneys should identify whether communication differences or difficulties may be a contributing factor in false confessions. Communication differences can be rooted in cultural misunderstandings or misinterpretation, such as linguistic and dialect differences between people of diverse backgrounds and law enforcement officers. Mental illness can also trigger cognitive and communication difficulties. This can impair mental processing, cause difficulty with comprehension, and impair ability to communicate effectively.[15]

Initial Hearing and Arraignment

Pretrial jail incarceration has significant negative health impacts.[16] People of diverse backgrounds across all racial demographics are less likely to be granted pretrial diversion compared to white people who have similar

---

13. Richard A. Leo, *False Confessions: Causes, Consequences and Implications*, 37 J. Am. Acad. Psychiatry & L. 332–43 (2009).

14. Lauren Rogal, *Protecting Persons with Mental Disabilities from Making False Confessions: The Americans with Disabilities Act as a Safeguard*, 47 N.M. L. Rev. 64 (2017).

15. Alice Medalia & Nadine Revheim, The New York State Office of Mental Health Family Liaison Bureau, Dealing with Cognitive Dysfunction Associated with Psychiatric Disabilities: A Handbook for Families and Friends of Individuals with Psychiatric Disorders (2002).

16. Traci Schlesinger, *Racial Disparities in Pretrial Diversion: An Analysis of Outcomes among Men Charged with Felonies and Processed in State Courts*, 3 Race & Just. 210–38 (2013).

legal characteristics.[17] This trend can cross over into other pretrial release opportunities. Jurisdictions vary in approaches to pretrial hearings and processes, bail and bond decisions, and other hearings at the start of criminal cases. Jurisdictions may appoint indigent or public defense at this point to those in need or may appoint counsel later in the legal process. Regardless of the appointment of counsel at this stage, attorneys should pay close attention to determinations made at pretrial hearings and recognize the impacts of pretrial detention.

The presence of a mental illness, on its own, should not be a reason for pretrial detention. It should not, on its own, be a reason to affix conditions to pretrial release decisions of any nature. If mental health information is known prior to pretrial release hearings/arraignment, it may inform release recommendations.[18] Release recommendations may require front-end diversion programs, pretrial release programs that mandate program participation in lieu of bail or supervised pretrial release with court-ordered conditions of release. Attorneys should request that the court individually tailor court-ordered conditions of release. Be mindful of avoiding recommendations that could violate due process and that may be medically or culturally inappropriate. Ensure that mental health information used when making pretrial release recommendations does not trigger negative impacts to pretrial release decisions or to the case at large.

Case Screening and Charging

The case screening and charging stage provides opportunity for prosecutors to make decisions that achieve fair and equitable outcomes. Decisions made here can impact reentry and return to the community, and these decisions can influence future health and recidivism outcomes. This stage allows prosecutors to decide the trajectory of future criminal justice

---

17. *Id.*

18. *See generally* CRIMINAL JUSTICE STANDARDS PRETRIAL RELEASE § 4-1.1 *et seq.* (AM. BAR ASS'N 2017); Hallie Fader-Towe & Fred C. Osher, *Improving Responses to People with Mental Illnesses at the Pretrial Stage*, THE COUNCIL OF STATE GOVERNMENTS JUSTICE CENTER (2015).

involvement, including who to remove entirely from the justice system and who should become more deeply involved.

Charging is discretionary, and prosecutors should consider the full range of charging options that can achieve the best possible criminal justice and health outcomes. Consider whether to file charges, whether charges will provide opportunities to connect people to mental health treatment, and whether charges will carry rigid penalties. Pay close attention to the amount or severity of charges, and the extent to which charges will cause unnecessary and unattended consequences. Identify which charges provide a gateway to treatment and which options hinder access. Review prosecutorial decisions to determine if trends in charging hint toward prosecutorial subjectivity or other factors that create imbalances. To give an idea of this, consider mandatory minimum sentencing laws. Under these laws, people of diverse backgrounds are likely to receive charges that carry heavier sentences than white people who share similar case characteristics.[19]

Consider collateral consequences as early as possible, and these considerations should begin at the charging stage. Collateral consequences can create long-term negative impacts. They can lead to poor and unmet health needs, negative housing and employment outcomes, consequential immigration decisions, and other enduring and sometimes permanent impacts. Collateral consequences severely impact people of diverse backgrounds.[20] Collateral consequences can cause people to experience worsened mental health and justice outcomes and deepened economic and structural inequities.[21] Attorneys should consider the collateral consequences of each potential charge. The following chapter provides additional detailed information about collateral consequences.

---

19. Marc Mauer & Nazgol Ghandnoosh, The Sentencing Project, Incorporating Racial Equity into Criminal Justice Reform (2014), https://safetyandjusticechallenge.org/wp-content/uploads/2021/06/incorporating-racial-equity-into-criminal-justice-reform.pdf (last visited Mar. 27, 2022).

20. Michael Pinard, *Collateral Consequences of Criminal Convictions: Confronting Issues of Race and Dignity*, 85 N.Y.U. L. Rev. 457–534 (2010).

21. U.S. Commission on Civil Rights, Collateral Consequences: The Crossroads of Punishment, Redemption, and the Effects on Communities (2009), https://www.usccr.gov/files/pubs/2019/06-13-Collateral-Consequences.pdf (last visited Mar. 27, 2022).

Attorneys should understand the impact of fines and fees associated with each charge and weigh the hardships that they may cause when making charging decisions. Fines and fees disproportionately impact people of diverse backgrounds.[22] Unaffordable fines and fees can exacerbate poor health outcomes and can cause stress and other behavioral health responses that trigger mental illness symptoms.[23]

Unmanageable criminal justice debt can cause economic and additional justice disparities. This includes the accumulation of debt that, left unpaid, risks further incarceration. Criminal justice debt can force people to decide between having fines and fees go unpaid or going without mental health treatment, medication, and other basic necessities such as food and housing.[24] Attorneys can intervene by analyzing charging decisions to ensure that any imposed fines and fees are punitive enough to deter crime while not so punitive that they cause unreasonable debt or poverty. Attorneys should also recognize that, while fines may help compensate survivors of crime for their losses, imposing unreasonable fines can backfire if people cannot afford to pay them.

Pretrial Conference and Plea Negotiation

Prosecutorial sentencing recommendations and initial plea offers can inform future sentencing decisions or eventual plea bargaining resolutions. Plea bargaining outcomes, however, can reflect racial disparities,[25] and mental illness may influence false guilty pleas.[26] Attorneys can use

---

22. U.S. Commission on Civil Rights, Targeted Fines and Fees against Communities of Color: Civil Rights & Constitutional Implications (2017), https://www.usccr.gov/files/pubs/docs/Statutory_Enforcement_Report2017.pdf (last visited Mar. 27, 2022).
23. Puja A. Upadhyay et al., Camden Coalition & National Center for Complex Health and Social Needs, Why Inequitable and Burdensome Court-issued Fines and Fees Are a Health Issue—And What Health and Policy Leaders Can Do about It, https://camdenhealth.org/wp-content/uploads/2021/12/CCH-Fines-Fees-Brief-Oct-2021-2.pdf
24. *Id.*
25. Berdejó, Carlos, *Criminalizing Race: Racial Disparities in Plea Bargaining*, 59 B.U. L. Rev 1187–1249 (2018).
26. Alison D. Redlich et al., *Self-Reported False Confessions and False Guilty Pleas among Offenders with Mental Illness*, 34 L. Hum. Behav. 79–90 (2010).

their role to avoid these disparities. Taking mental health needs into consideration during pretrial conferences and plea negotiations, when appropriate, is one step that can help achieve justice by creating pathways to mental health treatment, stability, and improved justice outcomes.

To be impactful, attorneys should recognize that jail and prison can cause severe harm to people who have mental illness, and that certain disposition options can inhibit access to mental health treatment. Attorneys should consider an array of available disposition options. These should comprise resolution through mediation when appropriate, available alternatives to incarceration, creative sentencing alternatives, and disposition options recommended by local advocacy programs or cultural groups. Plea negations should avoid requiring a guilty plea that sets people up for failure and easy return to jail or prison. Guilty pleas that entail cumbersome conditions can be difficult for people who have mental illness to comply with and can quickly return them to prosecution. Adopt the mindset that the best sanction or violation response is one never used. Consider mechanisms that allow prosecution to adjourn cases pending successful engagement in treatment.

To enhance pretrial conferences and plea negotiations, seek to understand people's intersectional identities when investigating the case. Creating a full picture can assist in determining which dispositions will be most effective and most responsive. Creating a full picture includes more than merely considering criminal justice and mental health histories. Examine family history, community engagement, and other factors that allow attorneys to fully realize the impact that disposition options have on people charged with crimes, their family, survivors of crime, and the public. Investigations should explore whether there is a nexus between mental illness and the circumstances associated with the alleged offense. This can identify unmet mental health and social service needs that, if responded to, can effectively deter criminal behavior and crime. When appropriate, it can be advantageous for opposing counsel to engage with each other to share investigation findings concerning people's background and to negotiate collaboratively to develop creative disposition options.

Competence to Stand Trial

People cannot be tried or convicted of crime if they are not mentally competent to engage in the legal process.[27] Serious mental illness may diminish one's ability to assist with one's defense or to understand criminal proceedings. In these situations, people may have difficulties in effectively communicating with attorneys or may refuse to engage with attorneys. Mental illness may cause them to distress or to experience memory deficiencies. They may have difficulty following the court process or be unable to understand abstract legal concepts. These challenges can raise doubt as to competence to stand trial. Incompetence to stand trial is not a legal defense, nor does it imply that mental capacity was a factor during the commission of the alleged crime. Unlike "not guilty by reason of insanity" defenses,[28] or other defenses where mental illness may be a mitigating factor in determining culpability, competence to stand trial focuses solely on the present level of functioning when moving through the legal process.

Doubt about mental competency to stand trial can be raised at any point during the trial process.[29] When attorneys or the court raise doubt about mental competence to stand trial, court proceedings are suspended, and people are evaluated to determine whether they are competent to proceed through the adjudication process.[30] The evaluation process is also triggered when doubt is raised concerning people's ability to move forward guilty pleas[31] or to waive the right of counsel and pursue

---

27. Pate v. Robinson, 383 U.S. 375, 378 (1966) (citing Bishop v. United States, 350 U.S. 961 (1956)). *See* Drope v. Missouri, 420 U.S. 162 (1975) (establishing rules that courts should consider any evidence that raises doubt to stand trial).

28. The term "insanity" is medically obsolete and considered a term that connotes legal terminology.

29. *Pate*, 383 U.S. 375, 378. *See Drope*, 420 U.S. 162 (noting the relevant circumstances that may require a trial court to inquire into the mental competency of the defendant).

30. *See* Dusky v. U.S., 362 U.S. 402 (1960) (sets forth a standard for determining competence to stand trial).

31. Godinez v. Moran, 509 U.S. 389 (1993) (competency to plead guilty).

self-representation.[32] For people who are determined competent following evaluation, their case resumes and moves forward through prosecution. For people found incompetent, their case remains suspended, and they begin the competency restoration process or are directed to other available disposition options set forth under state law. State law govern timelines associated with the competence to stand trial process, including timelines to return evaluation reports, opportunities for prosecution and defense attorneys to litigate report findings, and timelines for subjecting people to restoration services. State law also dictates available options, if any, for diversion from the restoration and criminal justice processes. State law designates legal processes that come into play if people are determined unrestorable or are not restored within statutory timeframes established to uphold due process protections.[33]

Attorneys need firm knowledge of mental competency laws and procedures. Attorneys should recognize when it would be appropriate to raise doubt about competence to stand trial, and when not to do so. Be familiar with available restoration services. Recognize that the goal of the competence to stand trial process is to return people to necessary mental functioning that will allow them to proceed through the legal process, and that the goal is not to establish sustained mental health treatment. Competency restoration may entail voluntary or involuntary medication,[34] but the competence to stand trial process is not a substitute for or a pathway to long-term mental health treatment and stability. Attorneys should practice cultural competency to ensure declarations of doubt about mental competence to stand trial are based on a mental illness or behavioral health need, and not based on cultural misunderstanding.

---

32. Indiana v. Edwards, 554 U.S. 164 (2008).

33. Jackson v. Indiana, 406 U.S. 715 (1972) (the nature and duration of restoration services must be in relation to the alleged charges).

34. Compelling involuntary medication for people found incompetent to stand trial raises substantive due process concerns. *See* Washington v. Harper, 494 U.S. 210 (1990) (finding that the Due Process Clause allows for involuntary medication for people incarcerated if their mental health condition makes them a danger to themselves or to others.) *See also* Sell v. United States, 539 U.S. 166 (2003) (sets limits on the right of lower courts to impose involuntary medication orders on people found incompetent to stand trial with the sole purpose of restoring competency).

Trial

Trial can be stressful for people of diverse backgrounds who have mental illness, and on attorneys. People of diverse backgrounds who have mental illness often face steep challenges in overcoming presumptions of guilt, particularly during a jury trial. They are also vulnerable to wrongful conviction[35] and vulnerable to being misunderstood based on communication and linguistic barriers that can harm decision-making.[36] While these disadvantages may be caused by systemic inequities, bias and stigma, cultural misunderstanding, and subconscious human factors, attorney intervention can mitigate their harm.

Mental illness and perceptions of race and culture can impact decision-makers, and attorneys have a duty to take action to mitigate unjust influences on decision-making. Mental illness can create cognitive and volitional impairments that impact behavior in the courtroom. Decision-makers can negatively construe those behaviors and form misguided judgments. People who have mental illness may appear disorganized, apathetic, emotional, or catatonic, or may exhibit inappropriate facial expressions or lack concentration. People may experience limited speech-language abilities or speak in a dialect reflective of cultural backgrounds that differ from those of judges or jurors. Decision-makers may presume them as guilty, find them unreliable, question their credibility, or falsely assume that they lack remorse.[37] Decision-makers, particularly jurors, may not believe in mental illness or may fear having people who have mental illness in the community, and may want them incarcerated rather than in the community with or without supervision. People of diverse backgrounds who have mental illness may face additional stigma and bias by experts and authority figures used as witnesses. Expert witnesses, arresting officers, and other officials can carry bias

---

35. *Dead Wrong*, *supra* note 12.

36. Taylor Jones et al., *Testifying while Black: An Experimental Study of Court Reporter Accuracy in Transcription of African American English*, 95 Linguistic Soc'y Am. e216–52 (2019).

37. *See generally* Judges' and Psychiatrists' Leadership Initiative & American Bar Association, Improving Cultural Competency: Working with People in the Criminal Justice System Who Have Mental Illnesses (May 16, 2019), https://csgjusticecenter.org/events/improving-cultural-competency-working-with-people-in-the-criminal-justice-system-who-have-mental-illnesses; *Dead Wrong*, *supra* note 12.

and stigma that can impact the case. Stigma and bias conveyed by expert witnesses and witnesses who are in positions of power may initiate or corroborate prejudicial thinking and beliefs held by decision-makers.

Defense attorneys should consider whether to advise a jury trial or advise waiver of a jury trial. Consider whether to raise mental illness as part of the case. Attorneys should consider the potential implications of disclosing mental health information in open court. Information provided in court may make its way outside of the courtroom and cause negative resulting impacts. These considerations may be contingent on the relationship between opposing counsel, the judge assigned to the case, the charges involved, and whether to raise mental illness as a mitigating factor.

Mental illness, on its own, does not presume to justify or excuse crime, and prosecution should not treat it as evidence to overcome. Attorneys should consider mental illness as a mitigating factor, including when there is and when there is not a nexus between mental illness and the alleged offense. Mental illness can help explain the mental processes and influences that led to the commission of alleged offenses. Attorneys should ensure that raising mental illness elicits understanding from decision-makers. Raise it when doing so will lead to reduced misunderstanding, fear, and other negative or punitive associations. It may be advantageous to walk decision-makers through the perspective of people who have mental illness. Walk decision-makers through what it is like to experience mental health symptoms and to live through those symptoms while interacting with legal and criminal justice systems. Walk decision-makers through the experience of what it is like to receive unresponsive treatment, and the experience of what it is like to then find and access culturally responsive treatment. Depending on the jurisdiction, state or federal courts may have special hearsay rules or exceptions that allow out-of-court testimony in certain circumstances that benefit the case while lessening the harm and retraumatization associated with providing in-court testimony.

As court processes change and shift to keep up with innovation, attorneys should additionally consider the emerging legal technology landscape and its impact on legal processes and the people involved with cases. Monitor the need for administrative intervention to reduce inequities. Court responses to the global pandemic of coronavirus disease 2019, for instance, created new short-term and permanent opportunities to host criminal hearings and trials remotely. While remote justice created advancements and innovations within the legal process, remote participation also created challenges for attorneys and other parties involved in criminal cases. To ensure equity, attorneys should discuss and troubleshoot with the court and with opposing counsel any anticipated challenges and fears arising out of remote appearance. People may face technology barriers such as lack of access to phones or computers. Technology barriers and limitations may risk interrupting private attorney-client communications. People may require special needs, and may need court interpretation, American with Disability Act accommodations, or other accommodations.[38]

Tools and Resources

- National Drug Court Institute Equity and Inclusion Toolkit.
- National Association of Drug Court Professionals E-Learning Center.
- *Improving Responses to People with Mental Illnesses at the Pretrial Stage: Essential Elements* by the Council of State Governments Justice Center.
- *Mapping Prosecutor-led Diversion* by the National District Attorneys Association.
- *Procedural Justice in Action* by the Center for Court Innovation and U.S. Department of Justice Bureau of Justice Assistance.

---

38. Michael Rempel et al., Center for Court Innovation, Learning from Crisis: Remote Justice in Criminal Courts (2021), https://www.courtinnovation.org/sites/default/files/media/document/2021/COVID_Remote_Justice_Criminal_Courts.Final_.pdf (last visited Mar. 27, 2022).

CHAPTER 8

Post-Adjudication and the Aftermath of Criminal Justice Involvement

This chapter continues the conversation about opportunities along the criminal justice continuum where attorneys can use their role to advance equity for people of diverse backgrounds who have mental illness. Focusing on legal processes post-adjudication and at the aftermath of criminal justice involvement, this chapter covers decision points during sentencing, determining entry into alternatives to incarceration, and at reentry. It reviews other legal and due process considerations that can come into play alongside and as a result of criminal justice involvement. While this chapter continues the focus on people charged with crimes, the following chapter discusses special considerations for witnesses and survivors of crime.

Sentencing

People of diverse backgrounds who are in jail and prison experience the highest disproportionately of mental illness compared to their white counterparts and compared to the general public. Looking at people of diverse backgrounds, they are more likely than white people to face charges that carry heavier sentences[1] and are more likely sentenced to prison.[2] People who are non-citizens of the United States are four times more likely than people who are citizens to receive jail or prison sentences in cases sharing similar criminal characteristics. They also receive longer and harsher sentences.[3] Factoring in access to mental health care while incarcerated, people of diverse backgrounds are more likely than white people to have their mental illness and treatment needs unaddressed.[4]

Connecting people of diverse backgrounds who have mental illness to culturally appropriate services at sentencing can enable them to achieve positive health outcomes while reducing their likelihood to reoffend. Jails and prisons can be traumatizing and may cause decompensation. People who have mental illness are often vulnerable when housed in carceral settings, where they are more likely to experience physical victimization than people without mental illness.[5] The stress of incarceration may cause them to exhibit disruptive behaviors that can cause facility management challenges for correctional and medical staff.[6] While jails and prisons are required to provide medical care to people housed in their facilities,[7] the mental health needs of people of diverse backgrounds are underserved or unmet. People of diverse backgrounds housed in jail or prison are more

---

1. Nazgol Ghandnoosh, *How Defense Attorneys Can Eliminate Racial Disparities in Criminal Justice*, The Champion 36–47 (June 2018).
2. John R. Sutton, *Structural Bias in the Sentencing of Felony Defendants*, 42 Soc. Sci. Res. 1207–21, 1214–16, 1218–19 (2013).
3. Ghandnoosh, *supra* note 1.
4. Melissa Thompson, Mad or Bad? Race, Class, Gender and Mental Disorder in the Criminal Justice System (LFB Scholarly Publishing, LLC 2010).
5. Cynthia L. Blitz et al., *Physical Victimization in Prison: The Role of Mental Illness*, 31 Int'l J. Law & Psychiatry 385–93 (2008). While there are no comprehensive studies that look at physical victimization of people who have mental illness in jails and prisons by racial demographics, there are studies that look at the interplay of physical victimization by race and other intersectional identities. *See, e.g.*, Sari L. Reisner et al., *Racial/Ethnic Disparities in History of Incarceration, Experiences of Victimization, and Associated Health Indicators among Transgender Women in the U.S.*, 54 Women & Health 750–67 (2013) (transgender women of color are disproportionately impacted by mental illness, incarnation, and physical victimization).
6. Fred Osher et al., *Adults with Behavioral Health Needs under Correctional Supervision: A Shared Framework for Reducing Recidivism and Promoting Recovery* 7 (The Council of State Governments Justice Center, 2012).
7. Estelle v. Gamble, 429 U.S. 97 (1976).

likely to not receive mental health treatment, or to receive mental health treatment at a higher, more restrictive level of care than is medically necessary.[8] Jails and prisons may also impose medical copayments for medical visits, treatment, and medication, which can cause financial hardships on people from traditionally marginalized communities or people who are indigent.[9] Upon release to the community, people may not receive a continuity of care between custodial and community health care systems. Lack of continuity of care can result in poor health outcomes and can contribute to recidivism.[10]

People facing low-level charges can be successful when connected to mental health treatment in the community instead of serving a jail or prison sentence. People facing higher-level and more serious charges and people with complex mental health needs can also be successful when connected to community-based treatment in lieu of incarceration.[11] In these cases, sentencing options should ensure connections to medically and culturally appropriate treatment, and connections to wraparound services that can respond to other needs. Wraparound services can address social determinates of mental health or criminogenic risks and needs. When incarceration is unavoidable, attorneys on both sides of the courtroom should advocate that people are housed in detention facilities that can respond to their mental health needs. This may be jails or prisons with specialized mental health units or facilities that have specific classifications that respond to complex health needs. Ensuring people are placed in detention facilities that can and will provide treatment at appropriate levels of care may reduce the likelihood of frequent facility transfers that interrupt the continuity of mental health care.

---

8. Thompson, *supra* note 4.

9. *See* Reynolds v. Wagner, 936 F. Supp. 1216 (E.D. Pa. 1996). *See also* Deanna M. Adams, *Copayments in Correctional Health Care: The Implications of COVID-19 and the Renewed Need to Consider Reforms*, in American Bar Association State of Criminal Justice 2021 (Mark E. Wojcik ed., 2021).

10. *See generally* State Fiscal Health, *Health Care Continuity after Prison Protects Investments and Progress*, The Pew Charitable Trusts (June 22, 2018), https://www.pewtrusts.org/en/research-and-analysis/articles/2018/06/22/health-care-continuity-after-prison-protects-investments-and-progress.

11. *See, e.g.*, Kenneth J. Gill & Ann A. Murphy, *Jail Diversion for Persons with Serious Mental Illness Coordinated by a Prosecutor's Office*, 2017 BioMed Res. Int'l 7917616 (2017).

Attorneys can assist decision-makers in determining the best possible sentencing decisions. Research the effects of various sentencing options on people of diverse backgrounds who have mental illness. Research the impact of jail and prison on people who have mental illness and available alternatives to incarceration that can promote treatment compliance and reduced recidivism. As part of this research, defense attorneys should seek a mental health evaluation and assessment and should consider whether to utilize a mental health expert or other witnesses who can provide information about various sentencing options.[12] The assessment and evaluation can provide context about the diagnosis, neuropsychological considerations, and any other physical or behavioral health needs. The mental health expert can also opine on the likelihood of positive outcomes through various treatment options, likelihood of success in available sentencing options, and other influential factors.

Bringing in a mental health expert who is familiar with the impact of incarceration and alternatives to incarceration on people of diverse backgrounds who have mental illness can help humanize them and can provide compelling recommendations on sentencing options that are responsive to their needs.[13] Mental health experts may also help develop a concrete treatment plan that would increase the likelihood of success if someone is sentenced to an alternative to incarceration program. Experts can help identify culturally responsive treatment providers, wraparound service providers, supervision programs, and other needs such as housing and transportation assistance programs. Bringing in supporting witnesses, such as a treating psychologist or psychiatrist, case managers, or family members, can provide useful information that can impact sentencing decisions.

12. *See* Ake v. Oklahoma, 470 U.S. 68 (1986) (establishes that, when the mental condition of a person experiencing indigence was relevant at the time of the offense and relevant to the punishment, the state must provide them with access to a mental health expert who, independent from the prosecution, is available to assist with the evaluation, preparation, and presentation of the defense). *But see* McWilliams v. Dunn, 137 S. Ct. 1790, 1799 (2017) (the Supreme Court has not stated whether *Ake* requires the state to provide a mental health expert who is available exclusively to the defense).

13. *Ake*, 470 U.S. 68.

Alternatives to Incarceration

Jurisdictions across the country are developing alternatives to incarceration at pre-plea and post-plea stages, and upon conviction. Available alternatives to incarceration may cover collaborative courts, diversion programs, probation or other community supervision, house arrest, electronic monitoring, and other options that combine court supervision with rehabilitative treatment and services. There are best practices for working with people who have mental illness and people of diverse backgrounds within the context of collaborative courts. These best practices extend far beyond collaborative court programs and are universally impactful across court proceedings and across alternatives to incarceration.

A firm understanding of research on alternatives to incarceration and alternative sentencing options can assist attorneys in advocating for placement in community-based programs that center around treatment and that address factors that led to the alleged offense. Empirical research on program success in similar cases can help establish a compelling argument as to why the program is an appropriate and effective sentencing option. Demographic and forensic research that looks at participant success across race and backgrounds can help educate decision-makers and opposing counsel on the effectiveness of community-defined practices or of programs designed for people of certain cultures. This is particularly crucial if programs are unfamiliar to or underused by decision-makers. Look at tribal services and restorative justice programs, for example. State and federal court systems often disregard and overlook these programs because decision-makers involved in those legal systems are often outside of the tribal community and unaware of program successes. These programs are effective in treating the behavioral health needs of tribal community members, reduce future criminal justice involvement, and enable them to engage in holistic practices that are meaningful to them and their community.[14]

---

14. Planning a Reentry Program: A Toolkit for Tribal Communities, American Probation and Parole Association & U.S. Department of Justice Bureau of Justice Assistance (2021) https://www.courtinnovation.org/sites/default/files/media/document/2021/Planning-Reentry-Program-Toolkit-for-Tribal-Communities.pdf.

A firm grasp on research can assist attorneys in developing compelling arguments for granting program access to repeat program participants. Research can inform arguments for program entry for people who have a history of unsuccessful program termination or who have successfully completed programs and later returned to the justice system. Prior unsuccessful program termination on its own should not disqualify program entry. Examine the circumstances surrounding the unsuccessful termination. Explore whether people voluntarily withdrew from the program, absconded, or received a program violation, or if new charges were filed. Consider what factors may have contributed to the unsuccessful termination. People may have unmet mental health or social needs that negatively impacted success. Program placement may have required services or programs that created barriers to success or required participation in services that were not medically or culturally responsive. Cultural unresponsiveness in programs such as treatment courts, for instance, contributes to racial disparities in program completions.[15] When reconsidering people for alternatives to incarceration, address barriers to previous successful completion so that people are set up for success.

Avoid artificially restrictive barriers to entry. Inequities can exist in alternatives to incarceration, including inequities stemming from program referral and eligibility criteria. Programs may exclude people considered high risk or who have multiple prior arrests. This can inadvertently exclude people of diverse backgrounds who are overrepresented in the criminal justice system and who come into contact with law enforcement more frequently than white people. Programs may also require people to have certain support systems that could restrict program access to people who have more unmet needs. Such criteria may require participants to independently establish stable housing, have access to private health insurance, or have the means to afford program or equipment fees. These criteria create a privilege for people of means and establish a system that punishes underserved people for their indigence or lack of resources.

---

15. Lisa M. Shannon et al., *Examining Racial Disparities in Program Completion and Post-Program Recidivism Rates: Comparing Caucasian and Non-Caucasian Treatment Court Participants*, 1 J. Advancing Just. 63 (2018).

These criteria exacerbate inequities and disparities impacting people of diverse backgrounds.

Consider the following questions when advocating for alternatives to incarceration:

- What alternatives to incarceration or alternative sentencing options are available? Would the case at hand qualify for available options?
- What mental health treatment needs impact the case? Are medically and culturally responsive services accessible? If not, what barriers are preventing access?
- What wraparound services will reduce the likelihood of future criminal justice involvement? Are culturally appropriate services accessible? If not, what barriers are preventing access?
- Are alternatives to incarceration or alternative sentencing options responsive to people of diverse backgrounds? Are they responsive to people who have mental illness?
- Are any modifications or special considerations—including cultural or treatment considerations—needed to ensure responsivity and success?
- What impacts—including positive, neutral, and negative impacts—will the alternatives to incarceration have on participants, the community, and the public?

Alternatives to incarceration referral processes may limit who can make referrals. This can expose program admission to biases and preferences. Subjective preferences can bleed into elements of the programs that impact responsivity and program success. People of diverse backgrounds often have lower program completion rates that are correlated to the lack of culturally responsive treatment providers used within the program.[16] Attorneys can intervene by reviewing eligibility criteria and advocating for changes that ensure equitable consideration across all potentially successful candidates. Attorneys can advocate to have program data reviewed

16. Timothy Ho et al., *Racial and Gender Disparities in Treatment Courts: Do They Exist and Is There Anything We Can Do to Change Them?*, 1 J. Advancing Just. 5–32 (2018).

regularly to understand treatment and program responsiveness and to identify barriers to success.

It is important to note that mental health courts should not be the only alternative to incarceration or disposition options considered for people who have mental illness. Mental health courts are great programs, and there are additional opportunities and programs to support people who have mental illness beyond the mental health court model. Mental health courts blend a treatment focus into the legal process. While mental health courts assist people in achieving positive health and justice outcomes, they have capacity limitations that prevent everyone in need from receiving them. People who have mental illness can be successful in other court and justice programs. Deflect people who have low-level charges out of the criminal justice system entirely. Connect them instead to mental health services in the community. For people not deflected, the black robe effect of mental health courts may be helpful for certain people, but others can do well without it. People who have mental illness can often engage in treatment without frequent court hearings to monitor compliance.

Community Supervision

When the court sentences people to community supervision, attorneys should recommend that the court consider their mental illness. Mental illness should inform the supervision itself, otherwise supervision conditions may set people up for failure. Advocate for supervision conditions that connect people to medically appropriate and culturally responsive treatment to the extent that treatment is appropriate. For instance, overburdening people assessed as low risk with supervision conditions can cause more harm than good. They are likely capable of positive change on their own, and imposing strict supervision requirements can cause them to become higher risk.[17]

---

17. *See, e.g.*, Douglas B. Marlow, *The Most Carefully Studied, Yet Least Understood, Terms in the Criminal Justice Lexicon: Risk, Need, and Responsivity*, Policy Research Associates, https://www.prainc.com/risk-need-responsitivity (last visited Mar. 27, 2022).

For others, mental illness may impair mental capacities or physical abilities, and may impact their ability to meet supervision requirements while fulfilling normal daily activities. In these situations, people can benefit from tailored conditions or treatment to assist with compliance in addition to regular activities. Conditions should respect cultural factors that can influence responsivity and engagement. Conditions should respect people's culture, practices, and beliefs, and people should not be forced into conditions that push religious or cultural ideologies that go against their own.[18] Attorneys should additionally be familiar with resources that supervision agencies have at their disposal, including resources required as a condition of supervision or as voluntary supports. Attorneys should advocate for special arrangements or assistance to ensure success. Consider these factors when examining facts surrounding a supervision violation and potential revocation should violation occur. Take, for example, people who benefit from assistance in tracking appointments, navigating public transportation, or finding employment. Connecting them to resources to assist with these activities will set them up for success.

Appeal

Attorneys should be familiar with the basics of appealing a court decision, including reversible errors that particularly impact people of diverse backgrounds who have mental illness. Ineffective assistance of counsel for not engaging a mental health professional may be a reversible error if mental illness and mental health history imply a need for a mental health evaluation.[19] It is additionally important to understand when to litigate relevant issues of race. These includes circumstances where racial bias influenced jury selection.

18. *See, e.g.,* Warner v. Orange County Dept. of Probation, 968 F. Supp. 917 (S.D.N.Y. 1997).
19. *Ake,* 470 U.S. 68.

Reentry

Reentry is not a solitary event. It is a process. Plan for reentry to the community following any length of incarceration as early in criminal justice system involvement as possible. Criminal justice involvement, especially when it results in a conviction, can create negative, long-lasting impacts if people are not prepared and not connected with services that will set them up for success.

Justice involvement can interrupt the continuity of care for people accessing mental health treatment prior to arrest, and it can put people on a trajectory for failure if there is not a continuum of care between jail and community-based mental health systems.[20] People reentering the community following incarceration have more medical, mental health, and behavioral health needs than the general public.[21] This is amplified for people of diverse backgrounds, who must overcome structural and health inequities in order to access treatment in the community or to maintain access to an appropriate level of care. Common structural inequities include limited or no access to mental health care or to culturally responsive care. Even if mental health care is accessible, treatment providers may hold stigma and biases against people who have criminal justice histories.[22] While attorneys must defer to the expertise of mental health professionals about treatment needs, attorneys can advocate for referrals to culturally appropriate providers. Attorneys can make informed referrals by considering the following:[23]

---

20. Jails and prisons may use third-party contractors that are unaffiliated with the public and private health systems that provide treatment in the community.

21. *See* April D. Fernandes, *How Far Up the River? Criminal Justice Contact and Health Outcomes*, 7 Soc. Currents 29–45 (2020); Ingrid A. Binswanger et al., *Health Disparities and the Criminal Justice System: An Agenda for Further Research and Action*, 89 J. Urban Health 98–107 (2012).

22. Sachini N. Bandara et al., *Mental Health Providers' Attitudes about Criminal Justice–Involved Clients with Serious Mental Illness*, 69 Psychiatric Serv. 472–75 (2018).

23. *See generally* Substance Abuse and Mental Health Services Administration, Improving Cultural Competence: A Treatment Improvement Protocol 59 (2014), https://www.ncbi.nlm.nih.gov/books/NBK207191 (last visited Mar. 27, 2022) (provides in-depth information that can assist attorneys in developing additional considerations for making informed referrals).

- What cultural beliefs does the person hold about the criminal justice system? What effect does criminal justice involvement have on the person?
- What beliefs does the treatment provider hold about the criminal justice system? What beliefs does the treatment provider hold about people who become involved in it?
- What differences exists between the person's cultural identity and that of the treatment provider?
- Does the treatment provider overidentify with the culture of criminal justice decision-makers? With the culture of correctional staff?
- What cultural groups does the person identify with when in the community? What cultural groups does the person identify with when incarcerated?
- What cultural attitudes and beliefs about treatment are important to the person?
- What cultural attitudes and beliefs about treatment are important to the treatment provider?
- Will the treatment provider integrate the person's beliefs, practices, identity, and cultural backgrounds into treatment?

Collateral Consequences of Criminal Convictions

Criminal justice involvement can carry adverse effects, and criminal convictions often trigger collateral consequences, some of which last indefinitely. Collateral consequences severely impact people of diverse backgrounds,[24] and can be detrimental to the health outcomes of people who have mental illnesses.[25] Attorneys should identify collateral or adverse impacts of criminal conviction as early as possible in the legal process and consult with people moving through the legal process to ensure they know what to expect as their case moves forward.

---

24. Michael Pinard, *Collateral Consequences of Criminal Convictions: Confronting Issues of Race and Dignity*, 85 N.Y.U. L. Rev. 457–534 (2010).

25. U.S. Commission on Civil Rights, Collateral Consequences: The Crossroads of Punishment, Redemption, and the Effects on Communities (2009), https://www.usccr.gov/files/pubs/2019/06-13-Collateral-Consequences.pdf (last visited Mar. 27, 2022).

Collateral consequences may require disclosure during criminal proceedings, while others do not and are realized after people have fully existed the justice system. Collateral consequences are wide ranging. They can impact people's ability to obtain certain licensures or to pursue certain career paths, for instance, or impact eligibility to receive government-assisted housing or public health and financial benefits. People may experience collateral consequences based on the length of stay in jail and prison, even if charges are dismissed or the case does not lead to a conviction.

Attorneys should consult state and local laws, policies, and processes when reviewing cases to identify potential collateral consequences. Identify collateral consequences that may particularly disenfranchise or otherwise harm people of diverse backgrounds, such as consequences that can jeopardize their livelihood or jeopardize their ability to fully engage with their community. Consider adjusting charges or sentencing recommendations to avoid inequitable consequences. When appropriate, attorneys should work with people to address collateral consequences as they near release from incarceration and exit from the criminal justice system. Attorneys can consult governing authorities through personal legal research or consult available repositories or databases that compile collateral consequences of convictions. Attorneys can also refer people to reentry counsel or legal aid societies to assist them with navigating collateral consequences or with appealing consequences through available civil legal or administrative processes.

Conservatorships

Conservatorships place people in court-ordered supervision based on their mental illness or other capacities that render them incapacitated.[26] Typically managed through civil legal systems, there are scenarios that can

26. State statute and case law set forth criteria for conservatorships. *See* Mathews v. Eldridge, 424 U.S. 319 (1976) (sets forth a test for when state action impedes constitutionally protected liberties. It implies procedural due process in any matter where government action would deprive people of liberty or property interest within the meaning of the due process clause of the Fifth and Fourteenth Amendments.).

route people involved in the criminal justice system into civil conservatorship processes or cause civil and criminal legal systems to have concurrent jurisdiction over the case. Conservatorships may include placement in a locked setting and may incorporate involuntary treatment orders in community and/or custodial settings.

The types of conservatorships available to people involved in the criminal justice system vary by state, and state statute and/or caselaw stipulate admittance criteria. A thorough review of available conservatorship types will broaden attorneys' understanding of potential criminal case outcomes that may include conservatorship. Conservatorship types can fall under three broad scenarios: (1) conservatorships related to current or recent criminal cases, (2) conservatorships indirectly related to recent or past criminal justice involvement, and (3) conservatorships for youth moving through the juvenile justice system or people who have cooccurring mental illness and intellectual and developmental disorders who are moving through adult or juvenile justice systems.

Conservatorships related to current or recent criminal cases may be a final recourse for people found incompetent to stand trial and, following the restoration process, who were determined permanently unrestorable. Conservatorships may extend to people released from incarceration or institutionalization following the completion of their sentence. These may be people whose mental illness is so severe that it raises considerable public health or public safety concerns. Conservatorships may be a final recourse for people found "not guilty by reason of insanity" and who remain severely impacted by mental illness. Conservatorships may extend to people whose mental illness was not a factor in the commission of the offense or in the conviction but who became permanently incompetent during incarceration.

Conservatorships indirectly related to recent or past criminal justice involvement may allow for conservatorships for people whose untreated mental illness causes them to be a danger to themselves or to others. Criteria may look at the frequency of arrests, incarcerations, or hospitalizations. Conservatorship may be a response for people who are unable to voluntarily engage in mental health treatment and their untreated mental illness causes them to be frequent utilizers of emergency services and criminal justice systems.

There may be circumstances where it would be more appropriate and in the interest of public safety to pursue conservatorship in lieu of criminal justice involvement. Attorneys can advocate for equitable outcomes by examining the factors used to make determinations and identifying whether cultural factors, stigma, or biases may have driven decisions to continue the criminal justice involvement instead of pursuing conservatorship, and vice versa. To illustrate this, consider situations where there is a nexus between mental illness and the charged offense. People meeting qualification criteria for conservatorship are, instead, processed through the criminal justice system due to systemic or structural inequities. There may be cultural or linguistic misunderstandings, misinterpretations, or barriers that influence the way decision-makers interpret symptoms or people's depictions of their conditions. Decision-makers may apply undue weight to criminal histories that disproportionately impact people of diverse backgrounds, such as multiple arrests or frequent engagement with law enforcement. Decision-makers, including people responsible for filling conservatorship petitions or otherwise initiating the conservatorship process, may also bring assumptions or biases that inhibit the process. This can include falsely assuming people of diverse backgrounds are inherently criminal and belong in the criminal justice system, or falsely assuming that they are unable to take care of themselves and belong in conservatorships. Attorneys should examine whether qualification criteria for conservatorships create racial or socioeconomic disparities or disproportionalities.[27]

Attorneys should understand their role in conservatorship processes, particularly as conservatorships may be solely a civil legal process or may create situations where civil and criminal courts have concurrent jurisdiction over a matter. There may be conflicts of interest for defense attorneys

---

27. *See, e.g.*, Jeffrey Swanson et al., *Racial Disparities in Involuntary Outpatient Commitment: Are They Real?*, 28 Health Aff. 816–26 (2009) (a study found that New York State's Kendra Law, which places people in court-ordered assisted outpatient treatment, disproportionately impacts Black people. The Kendra Law admission criteria focuses on people who have multiple hospitalizations in public mental health facilities. Because Black people in New York State were more likely than their non-Black counterparts to access public health systems, and because non-Black people were more likely to access private health systems, the law caused Black people to be overrepresented in the court-ordered treatment).

to represent people in both criminal and civil legal processes. Even in solely civil processes, prosecutors and defense attorneys may have a role prescribed by governing authorities. Governing authorities set forth criteria for courts to appoint conservatorship, including parameters around who provides advocacy and who may bring forward a petition for conservatorship or who may otherwise initiate the process. If prosecutors or defense attorneys have a role in advocacy or decision-making, they should ensure that conservatorship proceedings and outcomes are free of inequity. Examine proceedings and outcomes to determine if conservatorships cause disparities or disproportionalities based on race, culture, or criminal justice histories.

There may be involuntary medication orders or other types of petitions and matters for court review that are separate but associated with the conservatorship process. Prosecutors, defense attorneys, or attorneys acting in other specified roles may be involved in those hearings and processes. State statutes may restrict who can file conservatorship petitions and petitions for involuntary medication under a conservatorship. Regardless of their role, attorneys should understand opportunities available to them to advocate for people moving through conservatorship processes. This may encompass leveraging relationships with people involved in the process to ensure services provided are culturally responsive. Attorneys should examine the extent to which any involuntary medication orders are culturally appropriate and petitioned from providers who have experience treating people of diverse backgrounds.

For conservatorship processes that allow civil and criminal courts to have concurrent jurisdiction over a case, attorneys should be familiar with any timelines or decision points that allow for dismissal of the criminal case. This can help mitigate collateral consequences of criminal conviction for people of diverse backgrounds who have mental illness. To demonstrate this, consider conservatorships following incompetency to stand trial and unrestorable determinations. There may be statutory guidelines that allow people to petition for dismissal of their charges. If people do not petition to have charges dismissed and they later successfully petition the court to end their conservatorship, the criminal case may be resumed, and people may be subject to prosecution as they are now determined mentally competent and able to face the pending charges.

Concluding the Criminal Justice Continuum

This chapter, and the one before it, covered legal processes that impact people of diverse backgrounds who have mental illness and who are charged with crime. The following chapter continues the conversation about opportunities to leverage the attorney role to ensure fairness and justice for people of diverse backgrounds who have mental illness. It moves away from people who are charged with crime and focuses on people subject to criminal victimization—survivors of crime—and witnesses.

Tools and Resources

- *Tribal Reentry Advocacy Guide* by Root and Rebound.
- *Planning a Reentry Program: A Toolkit for Tribal Communities* by the Center for Court Innovation.
- *Practical Considerations Related to Release and Sentencing for Defendants Who Have Behavioral Health Needs* by the Council of State Governments Justice Center.
- National Inventory of Collateral Consequences of Conviction.
- National Reentry Resource Center.

CHAPTER 9

Special Considerations for Witnesses and Survivors of Crime

Criminal victimization is a complex topic. There are variables that impact whether survivors of crime[1] want to initially come forward or want to continue through the legal process once involved. Survivors of diverse backgrounds who have mental illness must face these variables, alongside the added uncertainty of whether jurors, judges, and other decision-makers will question their credibility.

The race and mental health status of survivors are consequential to case direction and case outcomes. These factors are often more consequential than the race and mental health status of the people charged with crimes. Looking across these factors, people who have mental illness are disproportionately victimized.[2] They are disproportionately victims

1. The term "survivors of crime" encompasses survivors and victims of crime at any stage of recovery from their victimization. The term is intended to meet people where they are at and acknowledges that, for some, recovery is not achievable.
2. *Mental Health Myths and Facts*, U.S. Dep't of Health & Human Serv. (2022), https://www.mentalhealth.gov/basics/mental-health-myths-facts (last visited Mar. 27, 2022).

of all crimes[3] and are 6 to 23 times more likely than the general public to be victims of violent crimes.[4] The impact of race on victimization is different but similarly disparaging. While criminal victimization is proportional across racial demographics,[5] justice is unlikely for survivors of diverse backgrounds.[6] Race and victimization create a complicated paradox. Cases involving white survivors receive greater scrutiny and punishment compared to similar cases involving Black survivors. This paradox expands to case dismissal, even in instances where dismissal benefits people of diverse backgrounds charged with a crime. Take cases involving low-level charges. Cases with survivors of diverse backgrounds are more likely to be dismissed than cases sharing similar criminal characteristics but with white survivors.[7]

Race and mental illness impact more than criminal victimization. They also impact perceptions of reliability and credibility. People of diverse backgrounds who have mental illness are not taken seriously.

---

3. Michael Barnett & Paul S. Appelbaum, *Testimony of People with Mental Illness*, 61 Psychiatric Serv. 958–60 (2010).

4. Linda A. Teplin et al., *Crime Victimization in Adults with Severe Mental Illness: Comparison with the National Crime Victimization Survey*, 62 Archives of Gen. Psychiatry 911–21 (2005).

5. Rachel E. Morgan & Jennifer L. Truman, *Criminal Victimization, 2019*, Bureau of Justice Statistics of the U.S. Department of Justice 17 (2020), https://bjs.ojp.gov/content/pub/pdf/cv19.pdf (last visited Mar. 27, 2022) (Proportionality reflects the victim-to-population ratio. Victimization ratios differ, and are disproportionate, when controlled for individual factors, such as prevalence estimates and victimization reported to police.). *But see* 2019 Hate Crime Statistics, U.S. Department of Justice, Federal Bureau of Investigation, Criminal Justice Information Services Division, https://ucr.fbi.gov/hate-crime/2019/topic-pages/incidents-and-offenses.pdf (last visited June 9, 2022), 48.4 percent of single-bias hate crime was motivated by anti-Black bias in 2019.

6. *See, e.g.*, Danielle Sered, *Young Men of Color and the Other Side of Harm: Addressing Disparities in Our Responses to Violence*, Vera Institute of Justice (2014), https://www.vera.org/downloads/Publications/young-men-of-color-and-the-other-side-of-harm-addressing-disparities-in-our-responses-to-violence/legacy_downloads/men-of-color-as-victims-of-violence-v3.pdf (last visited Mar. 27, 2022).

7. Marc Mauer & Nazgol Ghandnoosh, The Sentencing Project, Incorporating Racial Equity into Criminal Justice Reform 17 (2014), https://safetyandjusticechallenge.org/wp-content/uploads/2021/06/incorporating-racial-equity-into-criminal-justice-reform.pdf (last visited Mar. 27, 2022).

Jurors, judges, and other decision-makers often consider them untrustworthy, erratic, impulsive, or unable to provide persuasive testimony.[8]

Utilizing the Attorney Role to Engage Survivors of Crime and Witnesses[9]

Survivors of crime and witnesses are influential parties to criminal cases. Attorneys should be objective and presume that people of diverse backgrounds who have mental illness are capable of providing reliable testimony. Embrace cultural competency and trauma-informed lawyering skills to ensure their full participation. Recognize that survivors of crime experience high rates of trauma. Legal protections designed to protect survivors and witnesses may fall short of preventing secondary victimization, and participating in the legal process itself can traumatize them or cause re-traumatization.[10] Treat them with dignity and respect, and allow them to feel comfortable in their engagement in the legal process. This will enhance their participation in the case and encourage them to participate in the legal process again if future victimization arises.[11]

Working with survivors of crime and witnesses begins before the first meeting. Attorneys should seek out advance information. Research them by asking them for information and by reviewing police reports. Consider

---

8. Alexis E. Carl, *Dead Wrong: Capital Punishment, Wrongful Convictions, and Serious Mental Illness*, 1 Wrongful Conviction L, Rev. 336–63 (2020) [hereinafter *Dead Wrong*]; Taylor Jones et al., *Testifying While Black: An Experimental Study of Court Reporter Accuracy in Transcription of African American English*, 95 Linguistic Soc'y Am. e216–52 (2019).

9. Many concepts covered borrow from ideas and approaches covered in Chapter 3: *Ethical Pathways to Advocacy* and Chapter 4: *Establishing Lawyering Tools for Advancing Equity*.

10. Alliance for Safety and Justice, Crime Survivors Speak: The First-Ever National Survey of Victims' Views on Safety and Justice, https://allianceforsafetyandjustice.org/wp-content/uploads/documents/Crime%20Survivors%20Speak%20Report.pdf (last visited Mar. 27, 2022) [hereinafter Crime Survivors Speak].

11. The Arc et al., Victims, Witnesses, and Defendants with Mental Illness or Intellectual and Developmental Disabilities A Guide for Prosecutors (2020) [hereinafter The Arc]; Trauma Informed Prosecution Presentation, Institute for Innovation in Prosecution at John Jay College of Criminal Justice, https://www.prosecution.org/s/IIP-Trauma-Informed-Prosecution.pptx (last visited Mar. 27, 2022) [hereinafter Trauma Informed Prosecution Presentation].

interviewing others who have worked with them, such as responding law enforcement officers or service providers who treated needs arising from the event in question. Consider if they have mental health, cultural, communication, or social barriers that challenge their engagement. Determine if they need logistic or administrative support, and address inequities that may impact the meeting.[12] This may be socioeconomic barriers that prevent remote engagement like lack of access to telephones or to the internet. They may have jobs and family obligations that limit their availability. They may lack access to reliable transportation and be unable to travel to attorney offices or to court.

At the first meeting attorneys should begin by introducing themselves and their role in the case. Explain the legal process and ways that survivors and witnesses will impact the case. Detail what they should expect pretrial and during trial, and explain what is expected of them. Describe key decisions and processes over the course of the case that will impact them, such as decisions to dismiss cases or decisions to prosecute.[13]

Attorneys should be strategic when assessing credibility. Practice patience. Guide conversations by asking open-ended questions, and adopt a relational approach to help build trust. Identify behaviors manifesting from mental illness or trauma. Avoid misinterpreting them and determine whether, if the case moves to trial, decision-makers may misconstrue these behaviors as signs of dishonesty or use the behaviors to question the validity of their statements. Address any inconsistencies in testimony should they arise.[14] Be mindful that inconsistencies in testimony may not be rooted in untruthfulness. Symptoms of mental illness and trauma can cause anxiety, discomfort in the situation, or other impairments that can affect memory and cognition. Support memory retention and recollection by asking open-ended questions and explore

---

12. *State Court Behavioral Health Series*, National Center for State Courts, https://courses.ncsc.org/course/behavioralhealth (last visited Mar. 27, 2022) [hereinafter *State Court Behavioral Health Series*]; Substance Abuse and Mental Health Services Administration, *Improving Cultural Competence: A Treatment Improvement Protocol* 59 (2014), https://www.ncbi.nlm.nih.gov/books/NBK207191 (last visited Mar. 27, 2022); The Arc, *supra* note 11.
13. *State Court Behavioral Health Series*, *supra* note 12; Trauma Informed Prosecution Presentation, *supra* note 11.
14. The Arc, *supra* note 11.

memory prompts that can help jog memories. Memory prompts may include showing photographs of the crime scene, a map of the scene, or other cues that can trigger recollection.[15] As gaps in memory can be a trauma response, attorneys should be aware that memory prompts can retraumatize and be prepared to de-escalate if necessary. People may benefit from proceeding slowly and may need to take breaks to de-escalate strong emotions or otherwise regain composure.

Engage survivors of crime and witnesses to seek out a complete picture of the crime, including beneficial details about events leading to it. Be prepared to understand their description of events even if there are factors that impact their ability to communicate. Besides the impact of mental illness and trauma, there may be cultural, linguistic, or language barriers between attorneys and the survivors and witnesses.

Be flexible when determining approaches for interacting with survivors and witnesses. Allow them to speak without interruption and to take their time when doing so. They may be unable to recall events chronologically or in a logical manner. Ask follow-up questions that will assist in filling in memory gaps and developing the full picture of events. Identify areas where other evidence can corroborate their statements.[16] Attorneys should also know when to provide breaks and when to stop conversations. Survivors and witnesses may be unable to retrieve full details in one meeting and may be better able to relay information if there are breaks in the conversation or if they have opportunities to speak with attorneys over multiple meetings.

The mental health histories of survivors and witnesses may come into question. Mental health histories may be an element of the case, important to the circumstances surrounding the crime, or called into question by opposing counsel. If mental health histories are raised, ensure that they are approached respectfully and are not used to reproduce bias or stigma about mental illness. As bias and stigma are amplified for people of diverse backgrounds, develop counterarguments if mental health histories are raised by opposing counsel as means to impeach witness credibility. Adopt this principle to personal litigation strategy. Avoid

---

15. The Arc, *supra* note 11.
16. Trauma Informed Prosecution Presentation, *supra* note 11.

using the presence of mental illness, on its own, as a method to challenge credibility and to impeach witnesses.

Attorneys should consider the impact that disclosing mental health histories in court can have on survivors and witnesses. Choosing to do so may deter them from participating in the legal process during the case at hand or in events of future victimization. Consider the scope of record requests and limit requests to cover only information needed to move the case forward. Be open about the ways their mental health histories may be used and listen to concerns they may have. Seek their permission to obtain information and be honest about circumstances where other criminal justice professionals may have access to the information. Opposing counsel, court personnel, and others involved in the legal process may gain access to retrieved records.[17] If people testify in open court, members of the public may become aware of their mental health information.

Disclosing mental health history is a reason people of diverse backgrounds who have mental illness may be reluctant to participate in the legal process. Past negative experiences with the criminal justice system, attorneys, and other criminal justice professionals may also discourage participation. Race and cultural factors can dissuade participation, as can fear for safety, fear of repercussion, fear or uncertainty of the legal process, trauma and trauma responses, and symptoms of mental illness. Attorneys should seek out the reasons why survivors and witnesses may not want to participate in the legal process. Approach these conversations with compassion and honest curiosity. Discuss the consequences of not participating. Consequences may include case dismissal, subpoena, and consequences if they fail to comply with a subpoena. Remain open and compassionate if they continue to be reluctant. Utilize motivational interviewing to guide them in identifying personal benefits of participating in the case. If the case moves forward despite their reluctance, prosecutors should explain why the case is moving forward and why doing so serves the interests of justice.[18]

Attorneys should empower survivors and witnesses to participate in the case. Empowerment looks beyond encouraging them to recount

---

17. The Arc, *supra* note 11.

18. The Arc, *supra* note 11; Trauma Informed Prosecution Presentation, *supra* note 11.

events to the attorneys and during trial. It also encompasses the practice of monitoring behaviors that may affect their participation and knowing when to pause or when to change the pace of pretrial engagements. Empowerment also includes strategically preparing for trial. Attorneys may need to convince survivors and witnesses to testify if they are reluctant or issue a subpoena if they refuse.[19] To prepare for trial, attorneys should explain the trial process and describe the roles of the different people who will be in the courtroom. If possible, take survivors and witnesses to visit the courtroom. Ensure that the courtroom has necessary accommodations. Determine whether the survivors or witnesses will need to have an advocate or support animal accompany them while in the courtroom or while providing testimony.[20] Determine the need for translation services.

Even if people are willing and competent to testify, the court experience is stressful and intimidating, and it can traumatize them. This can impact people's ability to communicate or behave appropriately while testifying. People may fidget, not maintain eye contact, be unable to speak with conviction, or experience other symptoms.[21] Consider whether to call expert witnesses to provide testimony about trauma and trauma responses common for survivors of crimes similar to the crimes in question. Expert witnesses may also help put cultural contexts around their trauma responses. Confirm whether applicable hearsay rules or exceptions may allow out-of-court testimony that grants opportunities for people to provide testimony without having to appear in court and risk retraumatization or decompensation.

Using the Attorney Role to Seek Justice

A final thought in ensuring equity for survivors of crime is using the attorney role to help them achieve justice. Learn what justice means to them. Learn what type of outcomes they wish to see come from the case. This can provide valuable insight about potential courses of action or

19. Trauma Informed Prosecution Presentation, *supra* note 11.

20. The Arc, *supra* note 11.

21. *Dead Wrong, supra note 8.*

strategies that attorneys can incorporate into the case.[22] Explore whether different case outcomes may cause trauma or retraumatization. Survivors of crime often prefer that the criminal justice system focus on rehabilitating people who commit crimes rather than punishing them. They often prefer that people who commit crimes receive shorter sentences, rehabilitation, treatment, and alternatives to incarceration over jail and prison time.[23] Seeking justice for survivors can also mean connecting them to supports. Justice for survivors may include connecting them to victims' services or connecting them to culturally responsive treatment and support services in the community. Regardless of what justice means to them, listen to survivors, and assist them in seeking justice.

Tools and Resources

- *Victims, Witnesses, and Defendants with Mental Illness or Intellectual and Developmental Disabilities A Guide for Prosecutors* February 2020 by the Arc, NAMI, and Prosecutors Center for Excellence.

---

22. *Id.*
23. Crime Survivors Speak, *supra* note 10.

PART V

Moving from Theory to Action

CHAPTER 10

Navigating Authorities to Advance Equity

Equity is necessary to the pursuit of justice. Equity must be pursued to achieve fairness and impartiality. Attorneys across roles and across stages of their career have opportunities to approach legal processes and legal reforms to advocate for and advance equity. Acting within the bounds of legal ethics and the law, attorneys can invoke change by interpreting governing authorities and administrative processes to make meaningful differences in reducing disparities and inequity.

Practical Evaluation Leads to Practical Strategies

A helpful place to start in determining where attorneys can effectively use their role to advance equity is by discovering each decision point where they have discretion or power to influence outcomes. Attorneys can create a strategic plan for incorporating equity within a specific case, as well as within the broader legal agency and criminal justice system. This can be done by developing a comprehensive understanding of policies and procedures impacting decision points within the legal process and the criminal justice system. Sketch out policies and procedures that come into play throughout the duration of cases, including those that endure long after case resolution. Conduct a decision point analysis and locate decision points and other areas where attorneys can directly act or use their role to inform or influence outcomes. Identify gaps and barriers in policy and processes that can inhibit the effectiveness of attorney action. Identify barriers that trigger inequitable outcomes for people involved in cases. Once identified, attorneys can plan proactively.

Conducting this exercise can involve using different types of evaluation guides. Logic models, for example, lay out a visual representation of how decision-making will operate.[1] Logic models illustrate the logical relationship between the problem or need being addressed, actions/decisions, outcomes, and impacts. They also incorporate awareness about assumptions and contextual factors that may impact decision-making and outcomes.[2] Another evaluation guide is mapping. Mapping the sequence of events and associated procedures illuminates what should happen at each decision point, what currently happens at those points, and governing authorities that drive or direct decisions.[3] Mapping can reveal opportunities where attorneys can exercise discretion, intervene, or otherwise leverage their role to incorporate equitable responses into each case or into the criminal justice system as a whole.[4]

---

1. National Institute of Corrections, A Framework for Evidence-Based Decision Making in Local Criminal Justice Systems Starter Kit, 5a: Building Logic Models, https://info.nicic.gov/ebdm/sites/info.nicic.gov.ebdm/files/docs/5a_Building_Logic_Models.pdf (last visited Mar. 27, 2022).

2. *See, e.g.*, *Logic Models: Practical Planning to Reach Program Goals*, Illinois Criminal Justice Information Authority, https://icjia.illinois.gov/researchhub/articles/logic-models-practical-planning-to-reach-program-goals (last visited Mar. 27, 2022); *Sample Logic Model*, U.S. Dep't of Just., https://www.justice.gov/elderjustice/file/958191 (last visited Mar. 27, 2022).

3. *The Justice System*, U.S. Dep't of Just. Off. of Just. Programs, https://bjs.ojp.gov/justice-system (last visited Mar. 27, 2022).

4. *See, e.g.*, Junaid Afeef et al., Illinois Criminal Justice Information Authority, Policies and Procedures of the Illinois Criminal Justice System (2012), http://www.icjia.state.il.us/assets/pdf/ResearchReports/Policies_and_Procedures_of_the_Illinois_Criminal_Justice_System_Aug2012.pdf (last visited Mar. 27, 2022); Wisconsin State Evidence-Based Decision-Making Policy Team, System Mapping Narrative, https://cjcc.doj.wi.gov/sites/default/files/files/Draft%20Wisconsin%20EBDM%20State%20Team%20System%20Mapping%20Narrative%20Report_121615.pdf (last visited Mar. 27, 2022).

Inventorying community resources is a useful guide to understanding other criminal justice stakeholders and their processes. Inventorying provides opportunities for attorneys to get to know resources and providers across communities. Inventoried resources should comprise providers and resources that are court ordered, those otherwise associated with or required as part of case dispositions, or those accessed through voluntary referrals made by attorneys.[5] Inventorying resources enables attorneys to review processes and decisions that go into why and how people are referred to each provider. It also assists attorneys in locating providers that are culturally responsive, located in the communities where people are returning, and can respond to people's individual needs.

While there are no right or wrong methods for choosing evaluation guides, attorneys should select guides that are practical to and reflective of their unique role. To give an idea of this, elected prosecutors and appointed public defenders may select guides that diagram policies, procedures, and impacts from a bird's-eye-view of the entire local or statewide criminal justice system. Attorneys in senior-level policymaking roles may select guides that focus on agency policies and outcomes. Line staff may select guides that allow them to focus on the legal processes involved in individual cases. Regardless of attorney needs or guides selected, be intentional in raising equity as part of the evaluation process. Consider the following questions when conducing the evaluation:

- What are the goals, assumptions, and intended outcomes for the process being evaluated? What are the goals, assumptions, and intended outcomes for each decision point?
- Do the goals, assumptions, and intended outcomes consider variables that fall outside of the central interest? In other words, do they take into consideration environmental factors, individual-level characteristics and demographics, and other secondary variables that can produce significant differences when looking across people moving through the legal process?

---

5. *See, e.g.*, Judges and Psychiatrists Leadership Initiative, My Community Resources, https://csgjusticecenter.org/wp-content/uploads/2019/12/My-Community-Resources-JPLI.pdf (last visited Mar. 27, 2022); *Criminal Justice Ministry*, Criminal Justice Ministry, https://www.cjmstlouis.org/community-resources (last visited Mar. 27, 2022).

- What legal authorities, administrative policies, or other procedures direct decision-making at each decision point?
- Do these authorities avoid the missteps of color and cultural blindness/neutrality?
- Based on the prescribed authorities, what impact does decision-making have on the different groups of people moving through the legal process?
- What areas of decision-making are discretionary at each decision point?
- Is discretionary decision-making prone to subjectivity or other factors that can be influenced or informed by stigma and biases?
- Is decision-making transparent?
- Is there system-wide or agency-wide data, or individual-level data, that provides insight into the effectiveness of current policies, procedures, or discretionary decision-making in advancing equity?

Formalize Commitment to Equity

In addition to evaluating and identifying opportunities to advance equity through the attorney role, attorneys should formalize their commitment to equity. As was described in the context of motivating people moving through the legal process to change behavior based on the way they talk about it, attorneys must employ a similar strategy. Approach inequity as more than an issue impacting the criminal justice system and the legal process. Name it as a problem. Identifying inequity as a problem stresses the need for strategic responses that achieve real-world solutions. Formalize the commitment to seek out solutions that help solve the problem of inequity.

Formalize the commitment to reduce inequities and disparities impacting people of diverse backgrounds who have mental illness across the criminal justice system. Reflect on personal approaches to criminal cases and reflect on approaches to improve governing authority and administrative policy. Attorneys can get an idea of this by borrowing and adapting examples used to formalize commitment to impact broader criminal justice goals. Consider racial impact statements. State legislatures across the country have introduced and enacted racial impact statements as a tool to project racial disparities in criminal justice legislation before the legislation is adopted.[6] While racial impact statements provide a report of projected harms, they can be more effective if they set forth measurable next steps. They should also detail projected harms to different subsets of the population, such as people of diverse backgrounds who have mental illness and people of diverse backgrounds who have other behavioral health needs. Next steps should consist of actions needed to mitigate negative impacts and harms in the event that legislation is enacted.[7]

Similar to racial impact statements, counties and states with unified criminal justice systems are enacting resolutions to commit to reducing the number of people in their justice systems who have mental illness.[8] Notable resolutions set forth ideals for moving forward, providing a blueprint for taking action that can assist jurisdictions in achieving measurable outcomes.[9] Adopted resolutions can be effective in advancing equity if they include a formalized commitment to measuring and responding to disparities that exist within local criminal justice systems. This can help ensure that people of diverse background are not overlooked or unintentionally excluded in responses to people in local jails who have mental illness.

States and local governments, and individual prosecuting and defense agencies, should formalize commitments to reduce the racial disparities and disproportionalities of mental illness in their criminal justice systems. These commitments should include next steps or action items that pledge implementation and provide a framework for measuring progress and outcomes. Formalized commitments should establish parameters to

---

6. *See* Nicole D. Porter, *Racial Impact Statements*, The Sentencing Project (June 16, 2021) https://www.sentencingproject.org/publications/racial-impact-statements (last visited Mar. 27, 2022).

7. *See* Jessica Erickson, *Racial Impact Statements: Considering the Consequences of Racial Disproportionalities in the Criminal Justice System*, 89 Wash. L. Rev. 1425 (2014).

8. *See The Counties*, The Stepping Up Initiative, https://stepuptogether.org/the-counties/#/ (last visited Mar. 27, 2022).

9. *See, e.g.*, *Stepping Up Initiative County Resolution Template*, The Stepping Up Initiative, https://stepuptogether.org/wp-content/uploads/2022/05/Stepping-Up-Resolution-TEMPLATE_FINAL.pdf (last visited Mar. 27, 2022).

avoid making blanket assumptions that efforts will impact the universe of criminal justice populations. They should set forth a specific commitment to review impact across race, gender, cooccurring behavioral health needs, and other intersectional identities and social need. Depending on jurisdiction characteristics, the review should also consider local occurrences of concern, such as crimes, charges, or mental illness diagnoses that disproportionately impact people of diverse backgrounds.[10]

Collaborative Decision-making

State and local criminal justice systems should convene and task a dedicated working group of decision-makers to focus on equity. Criminal justice coordinating councils or similar bodies can undertake system-wide, interdisciplinary approaches to advance equity for people who have mental illness. Criminal justice coordinating councils are forums that convene elected and appointed policymakers to collaboratively address issues facing local criminal justice systems.[11] The names of such bodies can vary by jurisdiction and are established by way of legislation,[12] local ordinance,[13]

10. For instance, people of diverse backgrounds experience high rates of psychotic disorder diagnoses, showcasing racial disparities. This is driven by clinical bias, cultural misperceptions, and other race and cultural factors. *See, e.g.*, Robert C. Schwartz & David M. Blankenship, *Racial Disparities in Psychotic Disorder Diagnosis: A Review of Empirical Literature*, 4 World J Psychiatry 133–40 (2014). People who have psychotic disorder diagnoses, such as schizophrenia, are often excluded from alternatives to incarceration by way of eligibility criteria, stigma around the disorder, or subjective decision-making. The racial disparities in diagnoses, combined with program admission decision-making, disproportionately exclude people of diverse backgrounds.

11. *See Criminal Justice Coordinating Committees,* National Institute of Corrections, https://nicic.gov/projects/criminal-justice-coordinating-committees (last visited Mar. 27, 2022).

12. *See, e.g., Criminal Justice Coordinating Council,* State of Georgia, https://cjcc.georgia.gov/organization/criminal-justice-coordinating-council (last visited Mar. 27, 2022).; Cal. Penal Code § 1230.

13. *See, e.g.*, St. Louis, Mo. Ordinance 71012 (2019).

memoranda of understanding,[14] or other formal commitments. These bodies should add to their mission a focused goal to study and evaluate strategies to reduce racial and mental health disparities. They should ensure that all efforts pursued by the body, including those beyond the specific race and mental health focus, are regularly evaluated to ensure they do not cause racial or health inequities among groups or communities in their jurisdiction.

Legislative Opportunities

State law is the driving force behind what attorneys can and cannot do to pursue justice. Oftentimes, state law defines what justice means. It dictates who can receive justice and the path that must be followed to receive it. This can be reflected across different stages of the criminal justice continuum, including pathways falling squarely along the legal process.

To illustrate, state law prescribes opportunities for courts to authorize pretrial release conditions. Most states allow courts to impose any reasonable conditions of release, and roughly half of states allow courts to order or authorize mental health treatment and referrals to service as part of release conditions.[15] Over one-third of states allow pretrial diversion for people who have mental illness that avoids conviction upon successful completion.[16] California,[17] Connecticut,[18] Indiana,[19] Mississippi,[20]

---

14. *See, e.g.*, Sawyer County Criminal Justice Coordinating Council, *Memorandum of Understanding Between Lac Courte Oreilles Band of Lake Superior Chippewa Indians and Sawyer County Board of Supervisors Concerning the Sawyer County Criminal Justice Coordination Committee* (Mar. 17, 2021), https://www.sawyercountygov.org/AgendaCenter/ViewFile/Agenda/_0317 2021-1438.

15. *Pretrial Release Conditions*, National Conference of State Legislatures (2016), https://www.ncsl.org/research/civil-and-criminal-justice/pretrial-release-conditions.aspx (last visited Mar. 27, 2022).

16. *Id.*

17. Cal. Penal Code § 1001.36 (2020).

18. Conn. Gen. Stat. §§ 54–56l (2018).

19. Ind. Code § 11-12-3.7-11 (2021).

20. Miss. Code § 9-27-1 *et seq.* (2019).

Nevada,[21] and Washington[22] have statutes specifically creating diversion for people who have mental illness, and California and Washington allow diversion for people who were found incompetent to stand trial.[23] Looking beyond the early stages of justice involvement, at least 20 states have enacted statutory authority specifically establishing mental health treatment courts.[24] Additionally, all states have mental health treatment courts or other types of collaborative or treatment courts that can benefit people who have mental illness.[25] Most states allow alternatives to incarceration. At least 40 states allow alternatives to incarceration as a response to community supervision violations.[26] Roughly a quarter of states allow mental health treatment and other behavioral health treatment as an alternative to revocation for supervision violations.[27]

What is often unknown about legislation that allows for alternatives to incarceration or that incorporates mental health treatment into criminal justice responses is the extent to which legislation effectively serves all who should benefit. Legislation should be created and implemented to reduce racial and health inequities. Those who have the power to effect legislation should map out legislation and decision points and undertake a point-by-point evaluation, such as using the methods described earlier in this chapter. Measurable data should be collected to ensure that

---

21. Nev. Rev. Stat. § 176A.250 (2021).

22. Wash. Rev. Code § 10.05.020 *et seq.* (2005).

23. Cal. Penal Code §§ 1370 (2021), 1370.01 (2022); Wash. Rev. Code § 10.77.074 (2019). *See also* Trueblood v. DSHS, No. 15-35462.

24. *Pretrial Diversion*, National Conference of State Legislatures (2017) https://www.ncsl.org/research/civil-and-criminal-justice/pretrial-diversion.aspx (last visited Mar. 27, 2022).

25. *See Adult Mental Health Treatment Court Locator*, Substance Abuse and Mental Health Services Administration, https://www.samhsa.gov/gains-center/mental-health-treatment-court-locator/adults?field_gains_mhc_state_value=IA (last visited Mar. 27, 2022); *Juvenile Mental Health Treatment Court Locator*, Substance Abuse and Mental Health Services Administration, https://www.samhsa.gov/gains-center/mental-health-treatment-court-locator/juveniles (last visited Mar. 27, 2022).

26. *Responding to Community Supervision Violations with Alternatives to Incarceration*, National Conference of State Legislatures (2022), https://www.ncsl.org/research/civil-and-criminal-justice/alternatives-to-incarceration-for-supervision-violations.aspx (last visited Mar. 27, 2022).

27. *Id.*

legislation meets this mission. Mechanisms for doing this should include the adoption of racial impact statements that include measurable action items and next steps to ensure equity and to mitigate harm. Legislation should be evaluated regularly. It should require that qualitative and quantitative outcome data is tracked, reviewed, and used to inform ongoing improvements.

Legislation should be leveraged to ensure that people of diverse backgrounds who have mental illness are granted equitable consideration and benefits. Legislation should not be a driver to reproduce or deepen inequity. This includes drivers of inequity that disproportionately impact people of diverse backgrounds and people who have mental illness, such as legislation creating collateral consequences of criminal convictions and legislation creating administrative hurdles for clearing criminal records. Reform policies that exacerbate or reproduce race and health disparities in both the criminal justice system and in the mental health system. Reform policies that create economic inequities. When legislation cannot be enacted or reformed, explore opportunities to use administrative policy and agency practice to correct inequities.

Opportunities in Agency Practice

Operating within governing authority and making the most of legislation, there are additional opportunities to evoke change and to strive toward equity on the agency level. Agencies should be proactive. Examine pathways to treatment and reduced recidivism. Examine pathways to criminal justice involvement across all communities, and identity communities that are overburdened by criminal justice involvement. Establish a plan to understand the drivers of criminal justice involvement in those communities and opportunities for agency response and intervention. Develop proactive relationships with the communities that agencies serve and seek to protect. Embrace and incorporate community-informed responses. Recognize the importance of administrative strategy and agency policy that are informed by the experiences and knowledge of people and communities disproportionately impacted by the criminal justice system. Invite subject matter experts and community-informed experts to design responsive programs and agency practices. Regularly evaluate agency practices, policies, and outcomes, and invite community input and participation. Compensate community-informed experts, community leaders, and community members who are brought in to inform agency practices fairly and avoid asking them for intellectual and emotional labor for free.

Consider and learn from models such as community prosecution, holistic defense, and proactive reentry programs.[28] Community prosecution is a proactive model used by prosecutor offices across the country.[29] This model promotes partnership with communities by working with community members to identify public safety goals and to develop strategies to prevent crime by addressing underlying causes of criminal involvement.[30] A proactive approach to criminal defense is the holistic defense model, which has been adopted by public defender and indigence defense agencies around the nation.[31] Holistic defense brings together an interdisciplinary team of criminal defense attorneys; investigators; social workers; and civil, family, and immigration attorneys. This interdisciplinary team provides representation and advocacy for the criminal case at hand while also addressing the circumstances that contributed to criminal justice involvement and the collateral consequences of conviction.[32] Both

---

28. The example models presented are illustrated for informational purposes only and do not comprise an exhaustive list of strategies that attorneys and attorney offices may consider using. These examples do not constitute an endorsement, and any use of these models is recommended to coincide with regular assessment and evaluation to ensure they are administered fairly and equitably.

29. M. Elaine Nugent et al., *The Changing Nature of Prosecution: Community Prosecution vs. Traditional Prosecution Approaches*, American Prosecutors Research Institute (2004), https://ndaa.org/wp-content/uploads/changing_nature_of_prosecution.pdf. *See also Community Engagement Initiative*, National District Attorneys Association, https://ndaa.org/programs/community-engagement-initiative/ (last visited Mar. 27, 2022).

30. *See* Thomas J. Miles, *Does the "Community Prosecution" Strategy Reduce Crime? A Test of Chicago's Experience*, 16 Am. L. and Econ. Rev. 117–43 (2014).

31. *Holistic Defense, Defined*, The Bronx Defenders, https://www.bronxdefenders.org/holistic-defense (last visited Mar. 27, 2022); *See also* The Holistic Defense Toolkit, The Center for Holistic Defense, a Project of the Bronx Defenders, https://www.apainc.org/wp-content/uploads/2017/08/Holistic-Defense-Toolkit.pdf (last visited Mar. 27, 2022).

32. See James M. Anderson et al., *Holistic Representation: An Innovative Approach to Defending Poor Clients Can Reduce Incarceration and Save Taxpayer Dollars—Without Harm to Public Safety*, Rand Corp. (2019).

prosecution and defense agencies recognize that reentry is an event and not merely a single point along the criminal justice continuum. Agencies are developing reentry programs on their own or in partnership with criminal justice stakeholders to prevent recidivism and achieve reentry success by providing services that address unmet health and social needs.[33]

To humanize the people involved in cases, adopt agency polices to understand the lives and perspectives of people of diverse backgrounds who have mental illness who are moving through the justice system. One of the best ways to understand the affects and realities of each disposition option is to visit each resulting location. Visit punitive facilities, such as jails, prisons, and state mental hospitals. Visit rehabilitative agencies, such as treatment providers that operate alternatives to incarceration programs or social service providers in the community.[34] Seek out opportunities to understand the different cultures and communities in the local jurisdiction. Seek out their concerns related to criminal justice, the legal process, and social determinates of mental health. Be proactive in working with community leaders to respectfully visit services and providers that support the day-to-day lives of people with complex needs who are overrepresented in local justice systems. [35] These immersion experiences should be pursued by individual attorneys and should be instituted through administrative policy directing attorney onboarding and ongoing professional development.

---

33. *See, e.g.*, The Tribal Defenders Office of the Confederated Salish and Kootenai Tribes' Flathead Reservation and Reentry Program; U.S. Department of Justice Bureau of Justice Assistance et al., Planning A Reentry Program: A Toolkit for Tribal Communities (2021), https://bja.ojp.gov/sites/g/files/xyckuh186/files/media/document/Planning-Reentry-Program-Toolkit-for-Tribal-Communities.pdf; *Reentry Planning Toolkit*, Root and Rebound, https://www.rootandrebound.org/resources/reentry-planning-toolkit/ (last visited Mar. 27, 2022); *The Transition from Jail to Community (TJC) Initiative*, Urban Institute, https://www.urban.org/policy-centers/justice-policy-center/projects/transition-jail-community-tjc-initiative (last visited Mar. 27, 2022).

34. *See, e.g.*, Fair & Just Prospection, Nearly 40 Elected Prosecutors Pledge to Visit Their Local Correctional Facilities (Nov. 25, 2019), https://www.fairandjustprosecution.org/staging/wp-content/uploads/2019/11/Prison-Visit-Release-FINAL.pdf.

35. *See, e.g.*, *An Officer and a Mensch*, Glide, https://www.glide.org/an-officer-and-a-mensch/ (last visited Mar. 27, 2022).

Opportunities in Administrative Policy

Continuing the theme of proactiveness, agencies should seek solution-driven approaches to case resolutions. Establish agency policy that presumes innovative approaches to prosecution and defense, including innovative resolutions across both prosecutorial and non-prosecutorial options. Embody a commitment in agency policy to work collaboratively with opposing counsel and adversarial agencies to address social determinates of mental health and key drivers of crimes through plea negotiations and sentencing recommendations. For prosecution agencies specifically, ensure that plea bargaining achieves fair outcomes and enact policies that require time for people to consult with their defense attorneys as they consider plea deals.[36] Across prosecution and defense agencies, evaluate agency decision-making to ensure the agency as a whole and individual attorneys are proven to advance equity across cases, regardless of case outcome.

Prioritize treatment and rehabilitation in the community over punishment. Cultivate a commitment to reducing disparity and inequity by establishing fair eligibility criteria for alternatives to incarnation. If eligibility criteria are established by legislation or through outside authorities, examine opportunities to utilize the influence of agencies or discretion of attorneys to yield equitable admissions. Examine admission and program outcomes, including reasons people may refuse program entry and reasons for program success and unsuccessful terminations. Develop agency policy that requires the regular review and evaluation of case outcomes in alternatives to incarceration as well as other case dispositions. Include outcomes where people were connected to culturally and medically responsive treatment and to needed social supports.

Measures for Equity

Data tells a story. Data assists attorneys in demystifying misconceptions about crime and criminal justice outcomes. It tells whether legislation,

36. Fair and Just Prosecution, Issues at a Glance, Plea Bargaining, https://fairandjustprosecution.org/wp-content/uploads/2022/02/Plea-Bargaining-Issue-Brief.pdf (last visited Mar. 27, 2022).

administrative policy, and individual decision-making are effective. Attorneys can use data to impact the overall system, to inform personal approaches to case strategy, and to improve the persuasiveness of arguments made in court. Data can also be used to combat juror and other decision-maker bias or stigma, and to combat misleading media coverage that sensationalizes and wrongfully sways impressions about mental illness and people of diverse backgrounds.

Approach data with intention, not as a hindsight. Design legal responses to be data forward. Identify the goals that responses seek to achieve and ensure that data is collected to measure impact.[37] Data should be specific and inclusive. General population data that aggregates race and other demographics masks differential experiences. Collect and measure data across racial demographics and intersectional identities. Allow data to reflect self-identification of race and other demographic categories, and avoid assuming race, gender, and other social labels about the people moving through the legal process. Collect this specific data across all decision points and other areas that provide telling information about decision-making.

When inequity gets measured, it gets managed. Design data to be comprehensive and beneficially nuanced to avoid pitfalls that limit interpretation. Pitfalls are illustrated when looking at early criminal justice race data. Early race data often only compared "white" to "non-white" people, or "Black" to "non-Black" people. Similar missteps happen when studying the prevalence of mental illness in the criminal justice system. Early mental health data focused on people at certain decision points, such as people found incompetent to stand trial or people receiving psychotropic medication while incarcerated. Without distinguishing a full array of racial demographics, intersectional identities, or decision points, data falls short of illuminating equities and inequities, as well as successes and failures. When looking at existing data or implementing processes for new data collection efforts, design mechanisms to ensure that the

---

37. *See generally* Marc Mauer & Nazgol Ghandnoosh, The Sentencing Project, Incorporating Racial Equity into Criminal Justice Reform 17 (2014), https://safetyandjusticechallenge.org/wp-content/uploads/2021/06/incorporating-racial-equity-into-criminal-justice-reform.pdf (last visited Mar. 27, 2022).

data being collected is reliable. Tracking reliable data is vital for achieving meaningful and measurable outcomes.

Avoiding Retrenchment and Dissonance

The pursuit of equity for people of diverse backgrounds who have mental illness is vital, and urgent. Equity must not be an afterthought, or a secondary concern to legal processes and criminal justice reforms. It should not be treated as a competing interest that is easily sidelined by other legal priorities. Attorneys must embrace the duty of ensuring that law and legal processes advance equity. This duty ensures that the role of attorneys and the application of law create progress and avoid dissonance. Without specific focus, dissonance ensues and people of diverse backgrounds who have mental illness fall through gaps in reforms and legal processes designed to benefit people like them.

Attorneys must be intentional in their work. They must seek progress and avoid retrenchment. Progress is made when the law and case outcomes pursue equity. Retrenchment counters those efforts, challenging, neutralizing, or undermining progress. Whether retrenchment is intentional or an unintended consequence, attorneys must safeguard the legal process and the people moving through the justice system from its repercussions.

Law defines the legal interpretation of justice. Without incorporating an intentional equity frame, the law fails to provide justice to people most harmed by it. It is the duty of attorneys to seek fairness and justice for them, and it is the duty of attorneys to advance equity.

Tools and Resources

- *Motion for Justice* by the Vera Institute of Justice and the Institute for Innovation in Prosecution.
- *Unlocking the Black Box of Prosecution* by the Vera Institute of Justice.
- *Responding to Community Supervision Violations with Alternatives to Incarceration* by the National Conference of State Legislatures.
- *Mapping Prosecutor-Led Diversion* by the National District Attorneys Association.

- *50-State Searchable Bill Tracking Databases* by the National Conference of State Legislatures.
- *The Clean Slate Clearinghouse* by the American Institutes for Research.
- *The National Inventory of Collateral Consequences of Conviction* by the American Institutes for Research.
- *5 Ways Prosecuting Attorneys and Public Defenders Can Use Public Health Data and Resources to Address Substance Use Disorders* by the National Council of Juvenile and Family Court Judges.

CONCLUSION

Where Do We Go from Here?

Cases involving people of diverse backgrounds who have mental illness can be complex and complicated. These cases interface with both criminal justice and mental health systems, and each system informs—and sometimes misinforms—the legal process. Attorneys involved in these cases must look beyond mere litigation. Attorneys must address issues of law and procedure while managing barriers stemming from stigma, bias, and misconceptions that impact cases and that stand in the way of justice. The chapters of this book can assist attorneys in balancing law and procedure with pragmatic approaches to address the social, administrative, and procedural barriers that can obscure justice for people of diverse backgrounds who have mental illness.

To put theories presented in this book into context, consider the following scenario.[1] Jay Doe appeared at the preliminary hearing facing a smattering of disorderly conduct, false statement to an officer, and indecent exposure charges—charges that carry penalties of prison time, hefty fines, and sex offender registry. Jay was 21 years old and Black, presented as male, and was unemployed. Presenting an athletic built, Jay wore shoulder-length dreadlocks and forearm tattoos. Jay had a short criminal history: a collection of minor traffic offenses, a misdemeanor

1. The facts described are based on a real case.

cannabis possession, and public intoxication charges. Jay sat quietly in the courtroom next to his public defender. They were challenging the sufficiency of evidence for charges resulting from an arrest in an affluent, predominantly white neighborhood miles away from the historically marginalized neighborhood where Jay lived.

Calls for service arising from the charges in question described Jay knocking on people's front doors while acting suspiciously, and law enforcement had arrived as Jay conversed with one of the homeowners who had phoned the police. Prosecution called witnesses to testify at the hearing. The arresting officer described Jay's behavior during arrest as erratic, threatening, aggressive, and, from the officer's experience dealing with people like Jay who exhibited those behaviors, likely influenced by illegal substances. The arresting officer noted that people similar to Jay's description were not common to the neighborhood and that he found Jay's reason for being in the neighborhood unlikely. Homeowners who witnessed events prior to Jay's arrest described his behavior as bizarre, suspicious, and intimidating. They described Jay as being a noticeable outsider and expressed fear of him robbing or attacking them. The homeowner who interacted with Jay when law enforcement arrived on the scene gave a similar description. The homeowner also described Jay as unclothed, fidgety, and not making eye contact, and stated that he had made unusual requests of the homeowner.

As witnesses had described, Jay was not from the neighborhood where his arrest took place. His demographics, physical appearance, and life experiences were each on their own different from the people who resided in that neighborhood. Jay lived in a majority Black and brown community with his mother—a single mother who worked hard to move Jay and herself into a better area. The move came after Jay was held up at gunpoint while he walked home from work and, a short period of time thereafter, after witnessing a homicide. Jay was a high school graduate and, until quitting his job after the hold up, had worked retail and food service jobs throughout high school and after graduation to help his mother with living expenses.

Jay was soft spoken. Whenever he spoke, he used slang and vernacular common to Black adults his age who lived in his community. Also common to his community, Jay was well versed in the unwritten rules for conducting oneself when approached by law enforcement. His first interaction with law enforcement was as a high schooler studying at a public library, when a fellow patron made a call for service about a suspicious man loitering at the location. He had since stacked up experience interacting with law enforcement—through traffic stops, Terry stops,[2] witnessing the arrests of community members, hearing stories of unfair convictions from people reentering his community post-incarceration, and other similar encounters. These encounters instilled in him experience-based mistrust of the criminal justice system and experience-based fear of police officers, lawyers, judges, and the legal process. The case at hand validated Jay's mistrust and fears—through the circumstances surrounding his arrest, the time he spent in jail pretrial, and the minimal interactions he had with his public defender. Manifestations of an undiagnosed mental illness accompanied Jay's mistrust and fears. Although Jay exhibited indicators of mental illness, the indicators had gone unnoticed or misinterpreted by the criminal justice professionals with whom he interacted.

The prosecutor questioned whether substance use influenced Jay's alleged criminal behaviors, as described by the arresting officer and arrest report, or whether he had a mental illness. Following the preliminary hearing, the prosecutor requested that the public defender have Jay undergo a mental health assessment. The prosecutor had recently brought cases involving people who had mental illnesses and was becoming familiar with indicators of mental health needs. The prosecutor noticed indicators of mental illness based on witness testimony and from observing Jay in the courtroom. In a jurisdiction where arrests disproportionately impact people of diverse backgrounds, the prosecutor was also well versed in deciphering cultural misunderstandings and seeing through biased and stigmatized assumptions that commonly impacted cases.

Upon assessment, a psychiatrist diagnosed Jay with a mental illness. Jay was determined to be experiencing a high degree of severity, placing him in the serious mental illness classification of need. Given his age, degree of symptoms, and other details that emerged through

2. Terry v. Ohio, 392 U.S. 1 (1968).

assessment, Jay had experienced his first episode psychosis prior to arrest or had recently had his first episode but was never connected to a mental health professional until this court appearance. In the United States, a first episode psychosis—understood colloquially as a first "psychotic break" or the first appearance of mental illness symptoms—is experienced by approximately 100,000 people each year, with the average age of onset between 15 and 25 years.[3] Many people experiencing their first episode psychosis enter the criminal justice system before they receive mental health treatment.[4] Connecting people experiencing a first episode psychosis as quickly as possible to mental health treatment—early intervention—is critical for improving mental health and criminal justice outcomes. Like other people of diverse backgrounds who have mental illness, inequities and assumptions led Jay into the criminal justice pipeline rather than onto the pathway to treatment and stability.

A conviction in Jay's case would be life changing. Even without a mental illness, he would spend years in prison and, upon release, have fines and fees exceeding his ability to pay. He would be required to register as a sex offender, a consequence that would restrict his ability to find housing, find employment, and otherwise rejoin and participate in his community. His mental illness would trigger additional challenges, including the risks of decompensation and delayed mental health recovery. If convicted, there would be no guarantee for placement in a prison that could provide adequate treatment for his mental illness. There would also be no guarantee for connections to medically necessary and culturally responsive mental health treatment upon reentry. The totality of his mental illness if left unaddressed or under-addressed during incarceration paired with the consequences of his conviction would do little to achieve

---

3. Robert K. Heinssen et al., *Evidence-Based Treatments for First Episode Psychosis: Components of Coordinated Specialty Care*, National Institute of Mental Health (2014); Leah G. Pope & Stephanie Pottinger, *First-Episode Psychosis: Considerations for the Criminal Justice System*, Vera Institute of Justice (2017) 6, https://www.nasmhpd.org/sites/default/files/DH-First-Episode-Psychosis-Considerations-Criminal-Justice-rev3.pdf (last visited June 18, 2022), *citing* John McGrath et al., *Schizophrenia: A Concise Overview of Incidence, Prevalence, and Mortality*, 30 Epidemiologic Rev., no 1 (2008) 67-76.

4. Claire Ramsay et al., *Criminal Justice Settings as Possible Sites for Early Detection of Psychotic Disorders and Reducing Treatment Delay*, 65 Psychiatric Serv. 758–64 (2014).

a public safety "win" and would, instead, put him on the path toward further mental health instability and recidivism.[5]

The prosecutor in Jay's case, however, intervened and created an opportunity to change the narrative on how the case played out. The prosecutor acknowledged that conviction and incarceration are not always in the best interest of the public, and that alternative prosecutorial decisions often promote public safety and justice while responding to the needs of people charged with crimes. The prosecutor in Jay's case exercised discretion to defer prosecution in agreement that Jay serve a term of probation and comply with mental health treatment.

The scenario that transpired in Jay's case is only one example of using the attorney role to advocate for an equitable justice outcome. There will be many "Jays" involved in criminal cases—people facing criminal charges, survivors of crimes, and witnesses of crimes. They each will have unique experiences shaped by their mental illness, race, culture, and other intersectional identities. Their mental illness may be relevant to the facts of the case or may be an unrelated factor that attorneys must nevertheless respond to appropriately. Their intersectional identities shape their experiences moving through the criminal justice system and shape the ways attorneys, decision-makers, and other criminal justice professionals perceive and interact with them.

This book was designed to start a dedicated conversations among attorneys about the juncture of criminal justice, mental illness, and intersectionality. The pages of this book seek to aid those conversations by providing a collection of practical and straightforward tools and resources that any attorney can realistically adopt and incorporate into their practice. This book explores concepts of cultural competency and cultural awareness, as well mental illness, stigma, de-escalation, trauma informed

5. Jacques Baillargeon et al., *Psychiatric Disorders and Repeat Incarcerations: The Revolving Prison Door*, 166 Am. J. Psychiatry (2009). Mental illness on its own is not necessarily a driver of recidivism. The presence of criminogenic risks and needs, such as substance use disorders, in addition to a mental illness increases the likelihood of recidivism. Connecting people to mental health treatment and services that address criminogenic risks and needs can meaningfully reduce recidivism and improve outcomes. *See, e.g.*, James A. Wilson & Peter B. Wood, *Dissecting the Relationship between Mental Illness and Return to Incarceration*, 42 J. Crim. Just. 527–37 (2014).

lawyering, and motivational interviewing. It also illustrates opportunities for attorneys to leverage their roles to advance equity within individual cases and across the entire criminal justice continuum.

Attorneys: as you walk away from this book, use as many concepts and tools as applicable to your practice and to specific cases. Revisit concepts on a regular basis to find new inspiration or new areas of improvement that come to light as your practice evolves. You may find that certain theories or tools are relevant upon first read, while others prove enlightening once you are well versed in foundational concepts. You may also develop skills that surpass the bounds of this book or learn community-informed strategies that allow you to better uphold justice for the people and communities in your jurisdiction. As this book starts the conversation, use it as a resource and companion piece in your pursuit of equity and of justice.

A Final Deliberation: Disparity or Equity?

Attorneys have the responsibility to advocate for fairness and justice. Accepting this responsibility must involve recognizing that people of different groups are situated differently when it comes to systems and institutions. Attorneys must not be indifferent to the reality that people of diverse backgrounds who have mental illness particularly experience disparities and inequities within the criminal justice and the mental health systems. These experiences compound to influence the legal process and often obscure their chances for justice. Drawing inspiration from *Where Do We Go from Here: Chaos or Community?*, the final book written by the nation's most prominent civil rights leader, Dr. Martin Luther King, Jr., I reflect on the past challenges and accomplishments of attorneys striving for justice while combating racial and health inequities. With theories like therapeutic justice and trauma-informed lawyering, I place hope in the potential paths forward and hope for attorney innovation that will further advance the field. I nevertheless recognize that hope accompanied by inaction sacrifices justice. In the pursuit of justice, attorneys must do more than hope for equity and read about theories and concepts for achieving it. Attorneys must act.

Inequities that are avoidable, but not avoided, are unjust. People of diverse backgrounds who have mental illness—like their counterparts—have a right to receive fairness through the legal process and a right to receive the highest level of justice. Yet, they face avoidable inequities inherent to the criminal justice and mental health systems that legal processes can but often fail to address. Attorney intervention and action is vital to interrupting this failure and redressing injustice. Through the power of the legal profession, attorneys have the skills, passion, and creativity to bring about justice. Attorneys, I invite you to maximize your reach and seek opportunities in your practice to advance equity.

This is where we can go from here.

Recommended Reading

- Leah G. Pope & Stephanie Pottinger, *First-Episode Psychosis: Considerations for the Criminal Justice System*, Vera Institute of Justice (2017).
- Melissa Thompson, Mad or Bad? Race, Class, Gender and Mental Disorder in the Criminal Justice System (LFB Scholarly Publishing, LLC 2010).
- Social (In)Justice and Mental Health (Ruth S. Shim & Sarah Y. Vinson eds., 1st ed. 2021).
- Hillary Potter, Intersectionality and Criminology: Disrupting and Revolutionizing Studies of Crime (Routledge 2015).
- Judge Victoria Pratt, The Power of Dignity: How Transforming Justice Can Heal Our Communities (Seal Press 2022).
- Gregg Barak et al., Class, Race, Gender, and Crime: Social Realities of Justice in America (Rowman & Littlefield Publishers, 5th ed. 2018).
- Criminal Justice in Native America (Marianne O. Nielsen & Robert A. Silverman eds. 2009).

INDEX